Marriage/Self-Help/Relationships/Dating/Mate Seeking/Women Issues

This Is Why I Won't Marry You...

Why the Person You're Dating Won't Marry You

ARMANI VALENTINO

Cover & Interior design by Armani Valentino

Back cover photo taken by Chesa Starlette

http://www.armanivalentino.com

Published in Dallas, TX, by College Boy Publishing. College Boy Publishing is a division of The College Boy Company & ArmaniValentino.com.

College Boy Publishing titles may be purchased in bulk for educational, business, fund-raising, or promotional use. For information, please email collegeboypublishing@gmail.com. Or Call 972-383-9234

Autographed and wholesale copies of this book may be order directly from www.armanivalentino.com. Please allow up to 7–14 Business Days for delivery.

Armani Valentino is available for keynote addresses, workshops, panel discussion, radio & television interviews by calling **972-781-8404** or **armanivalentino99@gmail.com**

Printed in the United States of America

08 09 10 11 12 MVA 5 4 3 2 1

This book is dedicated to every single person that still believes in LOVE.

Be the Love you desire!

"Whoso findeth a wife findeth a good thing, and obtaineth favour of the Lord."

Proverbs 18:22

CONTENTS

INTRODUCTION

This Is Why I Won't Marry You is a book that I've been working on for the last 5+ years. It is the culmination of a lot of life lived, and of over 100,000 conversations with women and men from all walks of life, during that period. It is SPIRITUALLY based in some form, as are all of my writings. I assume that if you believe in the institution of marriage, you also believe in a Supreme Creator of all things!

While many people don't believe in a Supreme Source or Creator now-a-days, I do, and know the wisdom that has been left from many of the world's major religious or spiritual writings from the past. So, as in all of my books, you will find references to help me drive a point to something that I may have thought of, but later found it said a different way thousands of years ago, by someone else. As King Solomon said, "There is nothing new under the Sun." The purpose of this book is to get more people married and in loving and healthy relationships; especially those that have been dating or may have children together.

Why? Families are the cornerstone of our nation. However, over the years more and more individuals of marrying age are not getting married. The desire seems to still be there, but there are fewer marriages and more divorces than in the past.
About 1 million divorces happen each year. Therefore, I'm sure there is a fear in most people that they're relationship won't work. It seems much easier now-a-days for people to leave a relationship as opposed to being patient through the rough patches.

The following pages have been well thought out. From the time I first came up with the idea for this book, it's taken on a lot of different of phases. I've now simplified it to make it an easy read that will reach people around the world. All in hopes to answer the question in the minds of many...Why Won't They Marry Me?

Please read this book in full and with an open mind.

I hope you IN-JOY!

Armani Valentino

Marry YOU?

So you want to be married, but the person you are dating isn't sure they want to marry you. You don't know why? You're smart, funny, intelligent, nice looking, and you've been faithful.

He says he loves you and doesn't want to be with anyone else. You know he is not cheating, but he just hasn't popped the question. He may have already popped the question, but it's now 6 months or a year later and there is no set date on when you will be getting married. Or...the date is set but you're now feeling apprehensive about marrying him.

She has this list of this list (<---I meant that!), of everything you're supposed to be and do, and in your eyes you've lived up to this list. No matter how unrealistic this list has been you have done your very best at being every single thing on this list that she's had tucked away long before she met you.

Plus, you've been honest, a gentleman, nice, supportive, understanding, and everything else that she said she wanted you to be.

However, you're not feeling comfortable about asking her to marry you? So you have not bought the ring. Or...You may have bought the ring? She doesn't know you've bought it, BUT you haven't felt good about popping the question? Then again, maybe you did and she said, "No!" Maybe she said "Yes!" And...she's even been wearing the ring, but there is still some uneasiness inside of you about actually being with this woman for the rest of your life.

Better yet, the both of you may be feeling a little apprehensive about the fact that it may not last. You may be thinking "We may end up being one of the nearly 50% of first time marriages that don't work out." They may be thinking "One of these years just may be the year that we become one of the 1 million couples that get divorced each year in the United States."

However you slice it, it can be a lot to think about and very confusing. Either way, what a predicament to be in!

The Problem

As far back as history seems to go, there have been issues between men and women. The issues definitely seem to be those of opposed views, understanding, desires, and communication. Think about it...even Adam & Eve had relationship issues.

Today's man and today's woman have a whole lot to think about before making the decision to actually get married. The world has become smaller, more diverse, and the possibility that the marriage may not work has become statistically greater than ever before. The richest people in the world, most attractive, and most highly educated people in the world have just as many issues with relationships and love as everyone else; Thus, influencing even the most eligible bachelor and bachelorette, to decide to stay single.

At some point, I believe that almost every single man or woman that has a desire to be married has been in one or more of the situations mentioned above. All of these situations are real and may be the very reason why you are reading this book.

At the time that the idea for this book came about, I was getting over a 5+ year relationship with my college sweetheart, and finally dating again. I had started writing my now bestselling book, *99 Questions You Must Ask a Man Before Sleeping with Him & Definitely Before Having SEX*, and was dating another beautiful young lady.

Both she and I (at some point) thought that we were going to get married; just as I and the one before her had thought. The only issue was we went back and forth as far as who was ready at what time. For me, since I had previously been with the woman that I thought I was going to marry, have children by, and be with for the rest of my life, I was moving forward a little slower than she would have liked for me to.

The funny part about this is the same thing happened in my most recent relationship as well. I'll talk more about the importance of timing of marriage for a man later in the book.

Ms. Best Case Scenario

I believe that I am the marrying type. I can stay faithful, be honest, loving, caring, be affectionate, cook a little bit, work, etc. I'm not perfect, BUT...I'm also not looking for this perfect woman, and I don't think most men are. I do however; see many women waiting on what they call "THE ONE!" At a certain age in a man's life, I believe we realize that there is no perfect woman, and we just look for what is called, "Ms. Best Case Scenario!"

Ms. Best Case Scenario is a woman that may not be physically what we personally desire, but is what a man can see himself with long-term. She may not have the prettiest face, but she is nice looking and has a great personality, which makes her even more attractive than the woman that *thinks her shit doesn't stink*.

Ms. Best Case Scenario is a woman that a man accepts for where she is based on the life she has lived. She also is the woman that accepts him for where he is based on the life he has lived, and not where she thinks he should be. Men understand that Ms. Best Case Scenario just may be the woman that we need.
What I've found to be true is that what we need usually ends up turning out to be, what we actually want.

THE ONE

I mean come on now...in my lifetime I've met numerous women in their 30's, 40's, 50's, 60's, & 70's ALL TALKING ABOUT WAITING ON "THE ONE!" Some have been married, divorced, remarried 2 or three times and/or more, and are still talking about "THE ONE." Others have dated a whole lot of men, and will still tell you that they haven't married or found "THE ONE!" Really???

While this may be true in a few cases, the idea that ALL of the men you've dated or have ever been joined with aren't "THE ONE" may be the very reason why you're not married. Remember, you're the common denominator in each situation. Women want to be accepted and understood just as they are. Yet, many seem to be ***seeking perfection in an imperfect person.***

Women are awaiting the arrival of this guy on their list. This list doesn't have to be an actual list that she has created. Although, most of the time there is an actual list, just know that there is some kind of a list that you need to be aware of. And...the interesting thing is this list can be modified at any given time without prior notice. Therefore, "THE ONE" tends to change very often depending on the stage a woman may be in her life.

I, like most men understand when we meet a woman, most of time they will say something along the lines of, *"Well, I'm not looking for anything serious. Just want to start off as friends and see where it goes from there."* The other side of this is meeting a woman that says, *"I would like to be married and I date for the purpose of working towards a marriage."*

When a man hears one of these statements, if he is not ready to get married, he will stick with the woman that says the first one and run from the other; thinking that he has gotten away from commitment that leads to marriage.

What he doesn't know is, both of these women, no matter what the words are that are coming out of their mouth, ultimately want the same thing... COMMITMENT that leads to MARRIAGE!

Inside the Mind of a Woman that Wants to be Married...

There is a timeline in most women's mind that by a certain point in the relationship, certain milestones should take place. Here is the average woman's list of firsts'. Each of these depending on the woman will have a different time frame. If you are not able to keep up with the progression the way she thinks it should go, static will usually be created by her in the relationship about something that you may or may not even know.

- First date
- First kiss
- First cuddling session
- First time you come over to her place or that she comes over to yours
- First time you have sex
- First time you say I LOVE YOU

- First time you come to religious service with her or her with you
- When she should be able to meet your friends
- When she should be able to meet your parents or siblings
- When you actually claim her as your woman
- When you openly in public claim her as yours
- When you buy her an expensive gift
- When you first take her out of town/state/country/ road trip
- When you talk to her about marriage
- When you propose...

And all of that is just the beginning.

Women usually expect for you to know this, but of course we don't. Now-a-days in this I want everything right now mindset, in *WOMANDOME* you are supposed to make this happen within 12 – 24 months; especially for the woman over 30 years of age.

It doesn't matter where you are financially, spiritually, mentally or emotionally, she is expecting most of these things to happen; some will even speak against your manhood if you don't know this and may even compare you to another man or men, in attempt to get this from you.

Based on where they are in their own life, their own set of RULES, and the friends around them, a woman will express these desires in different ways.

We Are Different...

The approval of friends and family for most people is extremely important; especially for women concerning the man that they choose to marry. It can be very hard for a woman to separate their life into compartments. Therefore, a man usually has to be able to fit in this picture that they have created. If he can't and she really wants to be with him, she will try doing as most men absolutely do not like...SHE WILL TRY TO CHANGE HIM. If she sees that she is not successful at changing him, she will usually give up and move on.

Men on the other hand, when they find a woman that they want, they make their mind up and they usually stick with that when it comes to marrying her. They usually accept this woman for who she is and where she is in her life. His mother, father, siblings, and friends could all be against the decision. A man usually sees his choice for the woman he marries as a total separate compartment of his life. It's easy for him in most cases to separate lady, home, friends, extended family, and work more easily than his female counterpart.

A woman sees the relationship and her choice for marriage as a charter bus that has everything and everyone else on it already, and needs someone (husband) to drive the bus where she wants to go.

A man sees the relationship and choice for marriage as a sports car or a 4 door sedan. He is thinking, "I'm headed this direction. I have a seat for you right beside me and enough room for a few children (yours and/or mine OR both of ours in the future) in the back."

Men and Women are different. Scientifically, the way our brain processes information is even different. On average, a woman uses about 10,000-15,000 more words per day to express herself. Our differences are both natural and factual. As soon as we can realize and accept this, as opposed to trying to change one another, it will help us in our interactions and allow us to be more sensitive to the needs of one another. It will also help us to be happier within our relationships.

Marriage Material

In my bestselling book, *99Questions You Must Ask a Man Before Sleeping with Him & Definitely Before Having Sex*, I introduced the fact that...

EVERY MAN IS NOT MARRIAGE MATERIAL.

Many of the women that read the book agreed with this wholeheartedly. I now want to introduce this as well...

EVERY WOMAN IS NOT MARRIAGE MATERIAL.

What is marriage material? Well, depending on the individual, marriage material can be a number of different things. Let's take a look at the definition of ***marriage*** to see if we can come up with a general definition of MARRIAGE MATERIAL.

Merriam-Webster's online definition of the word ***marriage***:

1 - a (1) **:** the state of being united to a person of the opposite sex as husband or wife in a consensual and contractual relationship recognized by law (2) **:** the state of being united to a person of the same sex in a relationship like that of a traditional marriage
b : the mutual relation of married persons **:** WEDLOCK
c : the institution whereby individuals are joined in a marriage

2 : an act of marrying or the rite by which the married status is effected; *especially* **:** the wedding ceremony and attendant festivities or formalities
3 : an intimate or close union

However, generally speaking, marriage material consists of the following:

1. A person that has a desire or wants to be married.
2. A person that would like to be committed to the person that they are married to for life
3. A person that understands commitment & TEAM
4. A person that goes into the relationship with the purpose of fulfilling the vows they took
5. A person that wants to GIVE of themselves unselfishly to the other individual that they are married to and not only just RECEIVE
6. A person that loves, supports, honors, respects, and tries to be the best person they can be.
7. A person that knows he/she is not perfect, nor seeking perfection in someone else
8. A complete person, that is not looking to be completed by someone else
9. A person desiring companionship and holy matrimony
10. A person that is honest, loving, caring, understanding, and kind

So, the list is a list of what I consider to be MARRIAGE MATERIAL. Again, I say "what I consider." This is a very general list; however, most people that I have talked with desire these same things in a partner for marriage. As you can see, there is nothing on the list that says anything about sex, money, education, health, family, etc. Why? Well, the list above is the starting point for the definition of where we'll go from here.

A person that is marriage material is a person that absolutely wants to be married. If there is a person that absolutely has no desire to be married, something must trigger within this person that will cause them to have a change of heart. It's like trying to get someone that doesn't smoke to actually smoke a cigarette. You'll be hard pressed to actually get them to do take a puff.

Some people can't see being married to the same person for the rest of their life. This is almost as bad as the person that doesn't want to be married because if it is your desire to be married to one person for your entire life, you have to be real with yourself and just know that this person will probably leave you if you marry them.

If the person doesn't understand what a commitment is or has a different definition of what a commitment is than you do, this will cause problems throughout the relationship. Many people have to understand that relationships are a TEAM effort.

They have not been able to independently choose to be a part of a team where the rules are made up by them and the other individual. This is what marriage and relationships are all about. You and the other individual are able to make up the *rules of engagement* based on your own personal desires, agree upon these rules and move forward.

However, most people don't do this because we have never been taught to do so. You and the other individual must decide what you want from one another and be willing to give and receive that which you've asked and are being asked of, in order for it to be a healthy relationship of love, peace, joy, and respect. Not having a full understanding of the *rules of engagement* upfront before marriage or relationships of all kind, can cause issues when it comes to words such as agreement and commitment.

If you have never been a husband or a wife, you must understand that neither you nor the other person is going to know exactly what to do each day. If you have not had premarital relationship and communication counseling, you will definitely be getting what is known as OJT or On the Job Training. While this is good in some cases, most of the time, even in an actual career, this is not the way to be successful.

Many women seem to be able to tell me what a man's responsibility to them is, but can't seem to tell me their responsibility to their potential husband . A lot of good men I have conversed with will say to me,

"WOMEN WANT TO BE MARRIED, BUT THEY DON'T WANT TO BE A WIFE."

Chase vs. Pursue

I was having a conversation on Facebook with a female friend of mine that is very opinionated; but quite genuine. In short, the conversation went something like this:

Her: So, what's up with men not wanting to do anything and pursue a woman now-a-days?
Me: I don't think men have a problem pursuing; we just have a problem chasing.
Her: Well it's the same thing Armani.
Me: No, it's not. Pursue is where there is a known end of where I am going with this and what is expected of me. Then, when I perform what is expected of me, I receive that which I was pursuing. On the other hand, chasing is a game that I can't succeed at as a man because it constantly changes when you feel like it.
Her: Games are supposed to be FUN!
Me: True. However, they're not fun when the RULES KEEP CHANGING IN THE MIDDLE OF THE GAME.

When this happens, the MAN begins to look at the WOMAN like the kid that used to come outside to play with the rest of the kids, and when things didn't go according to the rules they made up in the middle of the game, they would say, **"Well, I'm gonna take my ball and go home!"** They would usually end up playing by themselves. And this is the way many relationships end up as well. The person that acts like this ends up playing by themselves.

Men that are *serious about being married* don't have time for uncertainties from you and apprehensiveness about things and people that really don't matter to the success of the relationship. I will reiterate again, A MAN SEES THE RELATIONSHIP AS A SPORTS CAR OR SEDAN. He is not concerned with transporting everything and everyone you already have on your charter bus.

A man has to be able to be content and rest his mind in order to be able to produce the lifestyle that the woman of his choice desires. When he constantly has to chase her, he can't produce this lifestyle because it takes up too much of his time, effort, and energy; all the things needed to produce the desires of his heart and hers.

If he has had to constantly chase you, as opposed to pursuing you, THIS MAY BE, THE REASON HE WON'T MARRY YOU!

As my friend and international music artist Sham Pain says, **"Women of today want to play HARD to REACH and IMPOSSIBLE to GET!** Then complain about being single but want a man."

The Law of Reciprocity

Some people are givers and others are receivers. Most of the time, you don't get both in a relationship. When you do get an even balance or fairly equivalent balance of both of these qualities in a relationship, the relationship is usually a very healthy relationship.

The person that actually wants to fulfill their own desires, and has a concern about the other person's desires as well, is the person that can actually understand fulfillment in the relationship. This is the kind of person that will be able to make it through the rough patches and actually LOVE WITHOUT LIMITS. It is the ideal situation when both parties are able to do this.

Marriage is a two-way street. If a person doesn't understand the LAW of RECIPROCITY, they are probably not MARRIAGE MATERIAL.

In social psychology, reciprocity refers to *responding to a positive action with another positive action, rewarding kind actions. As a social construct, reciprocity means that in response to friendly actions, people are frequently much nicer and much more cooperative than predicted by the self-interest model; conversely, in response to hostile actions they are frequently much nastier and even brutal.* (Wikipedia http://en.wikipedia.org/wiki/Reciprocity_(social_psychology))

It would seem as if the positive aspects of the Law of Reciprocity would tend to be the easiest part for most individuals in relationships to do. On the contrary, many people now-a-days seem to reward kindness with nasty actions and unkindness with even nastier actions. These same individuals seem to wonder why their relationships don't work out and no one wants to marry them.

Proverbs 17:13 states, ***Whoso rewardeth evil for good, evil shall not depart from his house.*** *KJV*

Many believers in the Faith of Christianity are very familiar with a particular scripture that states, *"Give and it shall be given unto you; Good Measure, pressed down and shaken together, and running over shall men give into your bossom."*

It doesn't say whether good or bad will be given to you. It only says, *"Give and it shall be given unto you."*

Every major religion of the world has similar sayings or scriptures that affirm the **LAW of Reciprocity.**

Therefore, one must be very careful about what they are giving; especially in relationships. Give what you know you deserve so that what you give must come back to you. It is LAW!

What Every Man Knows

Every man innately knows that he needs a woman. Every man knows that the woman is most important piece in his life besides his creator. Even God, according to the Bible, said that after he made man, he saw that there was a problem. What was the problem he recognized?

IT IS NOT GOOD THAT THE MAN SHOULD BE ALONE...

Now, whether a person believes the Bible as fact or not, MEN KNOW THAT WE NEED A WOMAN because it is NOT GOOD FOR US TO BE ALONE.

A man knows that he needs help. He knows that he needs a mate that can help him through this life. He needs companionship. Even his natural desire to be intimate with you is something that he really can't control because even in his physiological make up, he is geared to produce children for his whole life; once he starts puberty.

I recently saw a story on the news of a 96 year old man having a child. http://www.cbsnews.com/video/watch/?id=50133334n

I personally know a man that was a friend of the family that fathered a child when he was 70 years old. So, the desire put in him is not only for the perpetuation of the human race, but a knowing that even as a child, his mother (a female) is not a desire but a need.

This is the reason why a child that doesn't have his/her mother growing up can be a really disturbed child. I was at a store in college and there was the worst kitten that I think I had ever seen. I asked the store owner what was wrong with this kitten. He told me, "Its mother died." I understood then that the female was absolutely important to all life.

Because a man knows that he needs a woman, he will try to do what he can, depending on what he needs from you, to get it from you. This is why many men have become very GOOD at temporarily playing by the woman's rules when it comes to getting one thing WE need; SEX. Men, will lie, cheat and steal for this one thing. Other than the energy of LOVE, the energy of SEX is the most powerful energy in the Universe. Sex is the energy of creation. It is a very powerful desire and a natural desire in both the male and female gender.

Sex expression is a huge motivating factor for many men. When properly used, one can create masterpieces in any field. A woman must know how to use this energy and a man's desire to express this energy, to benefit herself and the man.

SEX and sexual expression may actually be one of the foremost thoughts on a man's mind throughout the day; especially if they recently started puberty or became sexually active. Research shows that men think about sex almost twice as much as women. http://www.psychologytoday.com/blog/the-sexual-continuum/201112/how-often-do-men-and-women-think-about-sex

A Woman Brings Balance & Stability

In November of 2011, I spoke at the Fabulous Women's Support Group's Annual Banquet. The title of what they asked to speak on was, "Finding the Queen in You." I asked myself, "Why would they ask me to speak on this?" After my answer came why they would, I immediately became flooded with word after word to speak on the subject.

I'll try to briefly put here in both a scientific and scriptural manner the importance of womrn as it was revealed to me after being asked to speak on the above topic. My mother is a science teacher so I have always been able to look at everything from a scientific, mathematical, and spiritual viewpoint all at the same time.

In the first Chapter of Genesis, in the 27th verse, the writer states something along the lines of *"male and female, created he, them both."* He then formed man from the dust of the earth in the second chapter, breathed into him the breath of life and man became a living soul. In science, the male sperm determines the sex of the child. The X represents the female, and the Y represents the male.

After this, as I stated earlier, he saw THAT IT WAS NOT GOOD FOR MAN TO BE ALONE. Therefore, man was given a gift of the WOMAN, taken from his own-self. In the scientific X & Y representations of the male and female the Y by itself is unbalanced and is actually an X with a piece missing or a RIB taken from the side.

A WOMAN BRINGS BALANCE & STABILITY TO A MAN'S MIND.

Man, by himself, as a biological representation looks like this...XY

If any little thing happens or he leans the wrong way just a little bit, he tips over.

Man with his woman or his helpmate in the biological representation looks like this...XYXX

If he tips over just a little bit, there is balance there in his female counterpart. Therefore, he is then able to stand firm. Without the woman, man can easily become unbalanced, unstable, unloving and hard.

The softer feminine and loving side of him, X, can easily be overshadowed by the harder male side Y.

From a scientific standpoint I see why those who believe in God or a Supreme Originator or Source refer to it as HE. Because by doing so, you include both the MALE & FEMALE.

Man was designed to multiply and replenish the earth and subdue it. It's very difficult to do it without the woman. Why? There is no real motivation to do so other than to conquer for the purpose of conquering. Men buy the thing we buy and do the things we do to care for, maintain, or show off and impress a woman or women.

If you want a man to marry you, you must know what he already innately knows; HE NEEDS A WOMAN. The question becomes, "Is it YOU he needs?"

Top 5 Reasons Why I Won't Marry You

To complete the book, the research that I conducted had to be completed first. I was waiting on the information contained in this chapter, in order to complete the book. I wanted to make sure that the women and the men are able to see that in our differences there is a lot of similarity with what we expect and what we desire.

Conducting this research led to me to the realization of just how much we as humans live from the past. Our past experiences may play the largest role in both our success and failure in our relationships.

Deal-Breakers seem to come about based upon situations from past relationships or our analysis of other relationships that we recognize as bad or actually caused serious pain of some kind.

Many times we don't know what we want, until we find out what we don't want.

Being able to know these deal-breakers before getting in too deep will save you and the other person a whole lot of problems, and save a lot of time.

In the charts below there are a few demographic stats from the survey:

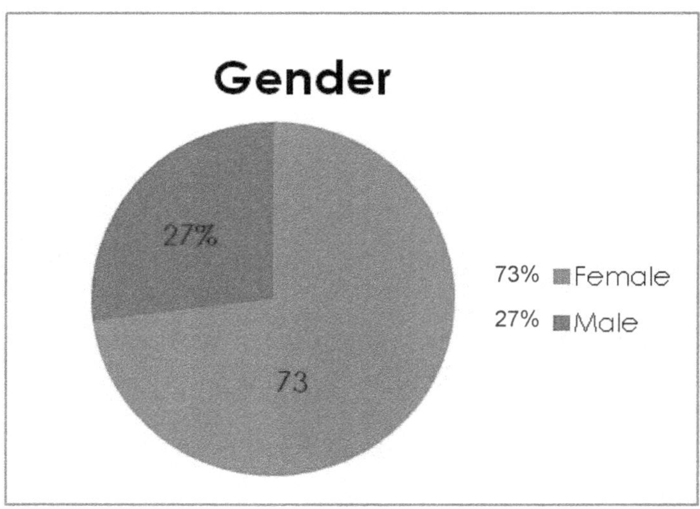

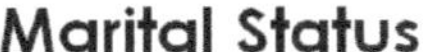
Marital Status

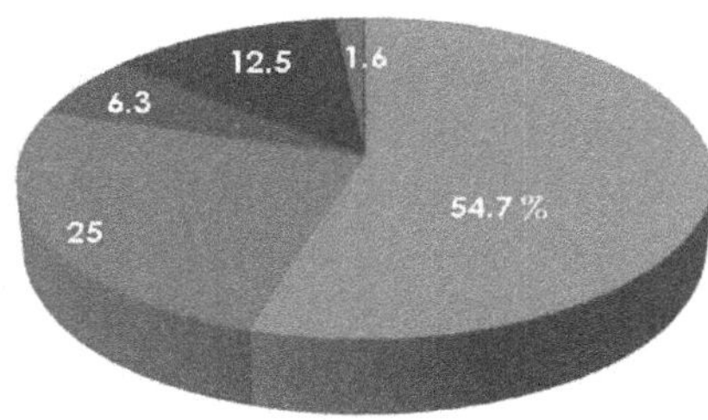
12.5
1.6
6.3
25
54.7 %
54.7 Single Never Been Married
25 Divorced
6.3 Seperated
12.5 Married
1.6 Widowed

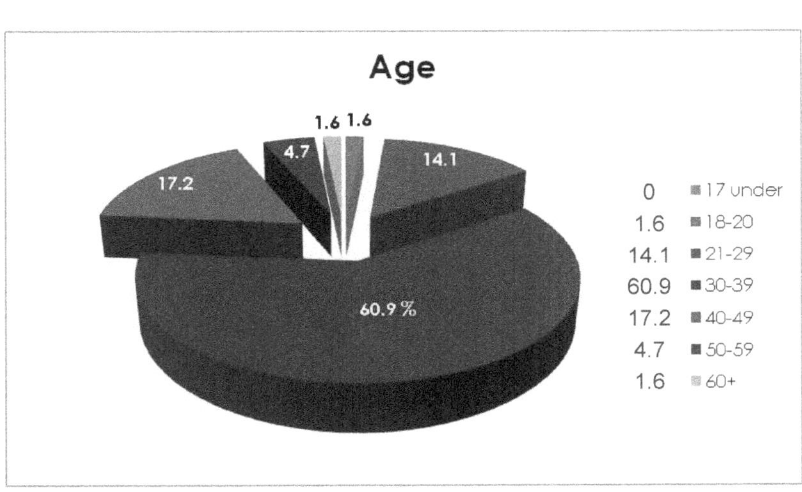
Age
1.6 1.6
4.7
14.1
17.2
60.9 %
0 17 under
1.6 18-20
14.1 21-29
60.9 30-39
17.2 40-49
4.7 50-59
1.6 60+

TOP DEAL-BREAKER
Men & Women AGREE
Lying, dishonesty, untrustworthy, not keeping your word, etc.

This was the top reason for both men and women. It's amazing to me that so many people can't seem to see that they are telling a lie. I know when I'm telling or have told a lie. I'm not a liar, but if I was to say that I have never told a lie, I would be lying. Some people have become habitual liars. Much like the character that Denzel Washington played in the movie *Flight*. They are living double lives. There is no transparency.

Others don't seem to see that when you say you are going to do something unless you let the other person or parties involved know something different, you pretty much told them a lie when you don't do it. One of the most common qualities of successful people is that their **word is good**. Meaning, when they say something you can usually trust it, or count on what they have said to actually become reality.

This is a trait that seems to not be very prevalent in the world today. If it were, less people would have listed this as their top deal breaker. Why do people lie? Who knows? I don't know. However, it's easier to just be congruent. While being positive is important, we must be careful to not become delusional. We can tell a lie for so long that the lie becomes our own truth; good or bad. Because of this, some people can become delusional about something that didn't actually happen.

For example, I saw a young lady on the Dr. Phil Show that had created a whole scenario about being pregnant. No matter what evidence was shown or what anyone else said, this is what she believed because it's what she created in her own mind. Therefore, to her it was REALITY.

I have actually experienced this with a couple of people before. It's like no matter what evidence you have presented to them concerning a situation and what actually happened, they have already created in their mind what actually happened. It's not the truth and even more so it's a form of psychotic behavior.

Lying is a failure method. The long term effects hurt the person telling the lie more than anyone else. Tell the truth. It works out better in the end by doing so. The ever so wise King Solomon wrote; ***16** These six things doth the LORD hate: yea, seven are an abomination unto him: **17** A proud look, **a lying tongue**, and hands that shed innocent blood, **18** An heart that deviseth wicked imaginations, feet that be swift in running to mischief, **19** **A false witness that speaketh lies**, and he that soweth discord among brethren.*

It seems that even thousands of years ago, lying was not a good thing and I don't think it will ever be an applauded characteristic. Even if you are not religious and have never been to any religious meeting, it is something or should be something in you that knows that lying is not a good thing to do. When I have told lies in the past, I never feel good about telling a lie.

#2 DEAL-BREAKER for Women Financially unstable, No Job, No desire for more, No Ambition

Say what you want about marrying a man for LOVE; women that responded to my TOP 5 Deal-Breaker's Survey, listed something concerning money, career, or stability more often and second only to lying, than any other reason.

While chatting with my friend Adetiba, I told him the results of the survey. He was a little surprised. His response was, "They (women) want to go on trips, buy new heels, charge money they don't have onto credit cards and look at a guy sideways if he doesn't have the money to "fix" her problems. They want the man to be Destiny's Child and pay their Bills, Bills, Bills." Then he laughed.

One guy said, "If you can't fix their problems, are frugal, or don't desire to waste your money taking care of them, you're cheap and not a real man. Go figure!" Another male said, "Women want everything right now.

They say they trust in God. But really they want you to be God. Ask and you shall receive. Then they're like "Oh you don't have it? Well go get it. This pressure for immediate gratification can easily force a man to engage in criminal activity."

On the following pages are some of the responses by women who took my TOP 5 Deal-Breakers For Marriage survey; concerning money/career:

- Bad with finances
- $$
- Lacking ambition
- Not financially stable
- Someone that is irresponsible/unstable
- He wasn't a provider aka no security
- No goals
- $$$
- Not financially sound
- Does NOT have a job or unwilling to work
- Cannot handle money....always want to party and smoke (whatever)
- Financially unstable
- Goals
- He spent more time frequenting bars and shopping and couldn't manage his finances
- Not being motivated or a hard worker.
- Financial
- Can't keep a job
- Moocher, leach, non provider
- Doesn't have a job
- Finances (listed multiple times like this)
- No drive or ambition
- Unable to manage finances
- You don't have purpose
- Poor money management
- He didn't want to work a normal job. He wanted to keep hustlin in the streets.
- Just haven't found a good independent man.
- Not being goal driven.
- Bad with Money
  blowing money
- He has no income of his own.
- No financial growth in the relationship

- NO goals ambition/ not driven -broke and broken
- Doesn't pay his child support. If you don't take care of your kids why would I even think you could take care of mine?
- Career reasons
- He's not stable enough
- No job (long-term) or aspirations in life
- Finances were not in order and no ambition to improve
- A deal breaker I have for not dating. Not goal oriented or vision minded. It's a marriage deal breaker by default because we would never make it through a dating/courtship process.

Many times, women meet a man that doesn't have a woman. A man without a woman is usually as I stated earlier in the book, an unstable man. Why? A man is trying to get a woman in his younger years. Therefore, his chase and/or pursuit to get established is usually not an easy feat. Once a man gets a girlfriend and is not in a constant chase or pursuit, he can then better court, plan and establish his vision. Once he decides to engage her, he is no longer DOUBLE MINDED. Remember, *"A double-minded man is unstable in all his ways."*

A woman helps a man to become single minded and therefore, usually able to become financially stable. Even if the woman is his mother, sister or friend, the motivation and inspiration brought to a man from a woman usually helps to bring singleness of thought,

and ultimately financial stability, security, and success.

This is the reason many women are attracted to married men. Married men usually have been able to create a financially secure lifestyle that is more attractive to a woman. They are able to see what he has gained materially because of the inspiration & motivation of another woman. They are also able to see his ability to deal with women in a different manner than a man that has not experienced dealing with the stress of a woman, children, house payments, car notes, and more. He has learned how to manage his life through practice and a *helpmate*.

According to Napoleon Hill, who exhausted 20+ years of his life acquiring knowledge about the reasons for financial success for men, the richest and wealthiest men had a woman that had inspired them to do so. He also found that the average man did not achieve financial success until he was around the age of 45.

I was having a conversation with my mother and she told me, "You're ahead of the curve Armani. No matter what your finances may look like right now, you're ahead of the curve, and you're going to be alright." Now, let me remind you that during this conversation I was having with her, I was totally struggling financially. One of the most influential persons in my life that I never met had just passed away, and I told her that he didn't write his first book until he was 49 years old. She said, "That's about the time most men get it together. Yeah, usually after 40. You'll be alright." She knew the same thing that Napoleon Hill knew. These words from my mother on that particular day helped me at a time I needed it most.

#3 DEAL-BREAKER for Women
Cheating & Infidelity

Women listed this in extreme amounts. While reading some of the comments that were left by women, I could almost feel what they were feeling. I often tell women that a man that is not married to you may feel that he is not cheating on you if he has sex with another person because you two are not married. This is the reason why I believe that it is very important for a woman to get married. Married men are less likely historically to cheat on their wife than cohabitating men, engaged men, and boyfriends that live separately from their female counterpart.

It is in the best interest of both parties to be married. Marriage is definitely protection for a woman that desires to lower the risk of being sexually cheated on.

I want to interject here that it is ok to get married and then have a wedding when you are in a better position financially to do so. *Don't let the fact that you can't afford a wedding be the reason you don't get married.*

Here are a few of them:

- "He wasn't living right"...meaning he couldn't stop cheating."
- Fear of being cheated on.
- He spent more time frequenting bars and shopping...
- Cheating *(listed multiple times just like this)*
- No self control (red flag for easily being tempted)
- Cheater *(listed multiple times just like this)*
- Divorced...my husband cheated on me.
- Tired of men cheating
- He cheated...three times
- Other women
- He was still involved sexually with his ex...
- He was still playing the field aka cheater

One thing I always like to remind women of is this, "Unless you are raped, a man can't have sex with you unless you open your legs." Meaning, as far as sex is concerned between you and the man, you are the one that has to submit to having sex with him. He is the giver, you are the receiver. Not having sex with a man or having sex with a man is a decision that you make.

Because people have been taught so much against having sex, that by the time many women get married, they may struggle with actually having sex with their husband on a regular basis.

'The husband should fulfill his marital duty to his wife, and likewise the wife to her husband. The wife does not have authority over her own body but yields it to her husband. In the same way, the husband does not have authority over his own body but yields it to his wife. Do not deprive each other except perhaps by mutual consent and for a time, so that you may devote yourselves to prayer." Corinthians 7:3-5 (NIV)

Being cheated on seems to be a big deal. So much so that it is mentioned in many of the ancient scriptures.

In this same chapter, in verses 1 & 2, the Apostle Paul wrote, *"It is good for a man not to have sexual relations with a woman. But since sexual immorality is occurring,* ***each man should have sexual relations with his own wife, and each woman with her own husband."***

#4 DEAL-BREAKER for Women
Not Believing in the same Religion, Lack of Spiritual Life, Disbelief in God or Attending Church, Not a Believer in Christ, etc.

This particular reason almost ranked higher than infidelity amongst women. While most of the women surveyed listed this is as a reason, it was not listed as one of the TOP (#1 #2 or #3) deal-breakers or more often as the other deal-breakers.

Without going into a deep discussion or getting into a religious debate, I was at an event speaking one time and this young lady asked the question, "I love a guy that is not the same religious belief as I am. What should I do?"

It was a very interesting question because I have experienced this myself. This particular young lady is a Christian. At this point, I asked her did she know what the Bible said concerning this and she said, "Do not be unequally yoked." I asked her, "Is that what the writer meant when he said that? Or did he mean something else?" She said, "I really don't know." I thought to myself, "Good answer." I then said to her, "Let's take a look at what is actually said concerning the marriage of someone that is not a believer or believes differently than you."

At this point, there were about 30 other people at this particular event that I spoke at. There was an evangelist that was the other invited guest speaker, and an ordained minister and married female of many years. I asked the both of them to please correct me if I am wrong at any time. They both agreed.

Now, I don't consider myself to be an expert of religion, but I usually understand words when I read them. I took her to the verse that she mentioned. I then asked her if he was an unbeliever or just believed differently than she did. She told me that he believed in

God, just differently than she did.

When people often use this verse of scripture as their reason to not marry someone, many women miss out on being married to a good man because of their lack of understanding.

After understanding the situation I immediately took her to a verse that was dealing specifically with marriage. 1 Peter 3 is concerning the wife submitting herself to her husband even if he was not a believer because in doing so, he may be won by her behavior. I then told her that the purpose of being a follower of Christ, from my understanding, was to win souls. I may be wrong, but I always understood it to be so.

If you are able to marry someone that has all the qualities you desire and you love them and they love you, in my humble opinion, you are not unequally yoked. My question always becomes, "If God is LOVE and LOVE is GOD, how can God/LOVE be unequally yoked?" I think the perception through what we have been religiously taught, causes us to make decisions not to marry based on anything other than unconditional love. But that's a whole different topic.

As many women and men find out, there are many who claim to be righteous or a follower of a particular religion and don't follow any of it.

As one woman told me, "He went to church with me all the way up until we got married. Shortly after

that, he stopped coming to church and told me he just did that because he knew it was what I wanted him to do. He didn't even believe in anything; let alone a different religion."

We all have choices. We all have the opportunity to choose the person that we would like to marry. Remember that our religion in most cases has been a choice as well. It is our relationship, not our religion that should define us and our character. As my friend Pastor Kelvy Matthews said, "It's about relationship not religion. And what people have forgotten or don't know – the relationship is a PERSONAL relationship with God."

When he said that to me over 4 years ago, I was in total agreement because God had already revealed the same understanding to me as well.

One lady told me that she could not be with me because she would have to submit to teaching that she didn't agree with. She said that she would have to submit to something that she never came to understand from the standpoint of an open mind. Again, to each his/her own. Just know that upfront and be real with yourself and the other person; and don't condemn a different belief than that of your own. It is not a wise thing to do.

When you approach any area of study, I was taught to always approach from the standpoint of being 100% objective. However, most people never approach anything, let alone religion from a non-biased place. They usually approach it from a place of trying to prove wrong or right, as opposed to learning something new.

I told one young lady, who was being belligerent at one of my engagements with other panelists & participants, *"If you listen, as opposed to thinking you already know, you might actually learn something and be able to get a man. Obviously what you've been doing hasn't worked for you."*

As I totally 100% believe, NO RELIGION IN THE WORLD HAS ALL THE TRUTH OF EVERYTHING. However, together, all of them may have the whole truth.

#2 DEAL-BREAKER for Men
Not being supported or
Negativity from a Woman

A man wants to feel supported, and a woman wants a man to support her. But when a man says, "Support me!" his meaning is usually a lot different from that of a woman. A woman usually means support her financially. So, when a man says this to a woman, her brain usually thinks he means the same thing she means when she says it to him. So, her response may be something like, "I'm not supporting you. You're a man. Support yourself."

When a man asks a woman to support him, he is usually saying, "APPREICATE ME, BELIEVE IN ME,

TRUST ME, ENCOURAGE ME, & BE HERE!"

When a man does not feel supported, he usually does not feel loved. A man needs to know that a woman will be with him through the storms, the peaks & valleys, and tough times that at some point are almost sure to come. As the group New Edition sang in their classic hit song, "Can You Stand the Rain?" A man needs to know that you are not with him when the weather or the forecast is only good. If every time something happens you flee and are nowhere to be found, a man cannot trust that you will be there and therefore, have not proven yourself bride worthy.

I tell women all the time, "Don't wait for the man to get 100% established without you and then want to be with him. Don't dog him out and berate him the whole time he is getting his footing in life together, and then expect for him to stick with you." This is a person of little faith.

Denzel Washington's wife supported him way before he ever made it BIG. He was a little short on the taxi ride on their first date, and she ended up paying for it. She could have really made a big deal about this as I've known many women to do. He was a man with a vision. She was a woman of vision as well. She caught hold of the vision, and to my knowledge hasn't had to work a job in years. Women want to enjoy the benefits of a stay-at-home wealthy woman, but have not invested the one thing a man needs from a woman; MORAL SUPPORT!

A Man of Vision definitely needs to know that

you can stand the rain. He needs to know that you have his back. If not, he will more than likely not be so eager to marry you.

One male respondent wrote: "*She failed to show me how much she loved me. She said it, but when time came to prove it, she would disappear or become distant.*" 10/12/2012 6:45 PM

#3 DEAL-BREAKER for MEN
Lack of Sex, Bad Sex, Infrequent Sex

Men listed sex as a very important factor in their choice for marriage. A woman that was not sexually satisfying was obviously a big deal. Infrequent sex was a big deal as well.

This is another reason to not have sex before marriage. The more people you have had sex with the more people you have to compare the next person to. One gentleman and I were having a conversation about porn and its effects on marriage, relationships and the family. I saw the benefit of it and the not so good benefits of it.

A man that does not enjoy having sex with his wife is not a good thing. It is not a good or easy thing to get over. A woman that doesn't enjoy sex with her husband is also not a good thing. The only difference for most women is that sex is more mental than it is physical. For most men it is definitely more physical.

So, when a man is no longer sexually attracted to his wife/partner, he is more likely to go outside the

relationship. There can be multiple reasons for this. One for sure is when she has been with another man. Another is after having to CHASE her versus pursuing her and still have not been given sexual reward. Sad to say, but sexual reward is high up there for a man that has committed to you. When he has been committed to you and you doesn't receive sexual reciprocity, he can eventually become very uninterested.

Sex makes most men feel like a man. Sexual addiction in men usually stems from this feeling of power that is received from it. Many men feel powerful through sex. The more enjoyable, frequent, and passionate that the sex is for him, the less time he even has to cheat with another woman. Not saying he won't but it sure helps to decrease the possibilities.

Plain and simply put, a man feels **<u>less</u>** loved when he is not receiving sex from his wife or woman that he has committed himself to.

#4 DEAL-BREAKER for Men
Cleanliness of Body & House,
Unhealthy Habits & Weight

I'm literally laughing as I begin to write this section of the book. This is one of my deal-breakers for sure. If a woman is not clean as far as her body is concerned, I cannot date her and definitely not marry her. I can deal with a not so tidy house, but if it is nasty as in filthy, that is a problem. I can be a little unorganized at times, but not filthy. A filthy woman is even more unattractive than a filthy AND unorganized man. I can be a little unorganized at times, so there is no way a woman that is as unorganized as I am could make it work. (Laughing as I write this.)

A woman should definitely keep her hygiene together. It is extremely important. Both men and women should bathe no less than once every 24 hours. I remember my grandmother taking multiple baths while I was growing up. I don't ever remember her leaving the house without bathing herself. That was over 20 years ago, and when I was having a conversation with my oldest sister, my oldest nephew was in grown folk's conversation and interjected. He said, "Yeah. Great-Grandma takes like 4 baths a day." Needless to say, his mom and I laughed really hard because we knew this to be true.

Not taking regular baths for men and women is very unhealthy. It is an unhealthy habit to form. It is unattractive. Another unhealthy habit that men listed is smoking and too much drinking. Men did not like to see a woman smoke. They considered this to be extremely unattractive. They also agreed that a drunken woman was even more unattractive than a woman that smoked; especially if she got drunk often from partying and clubbing with her friends or was a borderline alcoholic.

They also saw over-eating and obesity as a deal-breaker or unhealthy habit if the woman was not willing to make a change.

#5 DEAL–BREAKER COMMUNICATION, CONTROLLING, LACK OF COMPROMISE

Both Male & Female Agree

Communication is a very important, if not the most important gift there is in the world; especially during war. One of the first things soldiers are taught is to take out the communication towers or tap into the communication lines. This will cause confusion and allow for interception of battle plans.

In a relationship this is the same thing that happens. When two people are not communicating, it causes confusion and allows outside forces to infiltrate the minds of one or both parties involved. If you want to easily win a war without suffering lots of casualties, you get the soldiers to begin to fight and disagree amongst themselves. This will keep the morale of the soldiers low and weaken their ability to fight their enemy. When they keep doing this, they will kill the spirit in each other to fight the real enemy because their energies have been wasted fighting one another.

A united front is a strong front. Nothing is impossible when two people agree. One decided mind can put 1,000 to flight, but 2 people united can put 10,000 to flight. According to Matthew, Jesus said, ***"Again I say unto you, that if two of you shall agree on earth as touching any thing that they shall ask, it shall be done for them of my Father which is in heaven."***

The goal of communication is to understand and to be understood. Many times in a relationship one or both parties is not concerned with what the other person has to actually say. They are only concerned with proving the other person wrong, trying to pick apart what the other person is saying, or being the one that's understood.

The communication between two people or more can easily turn into an argument when one or both parties does not respect the other person enough to actually listen. Often, people do not hear the whole matter out before replying to the other person. They are thinking about what they want to say back to the other person as opposed to ACTIVELY LISTENING.

Active listening skills have to be taught. People aren't just born with these active listening skills. Most people never develop active listening skills. Active listening skills require one to almost nonresistant to the sender of the message, in order to receive the message clearly and in its entirety.

So much so, that there have been times when people have not read the whole of my books and will read a paragraph and say, "I don't agree with this!" I usually will tell them, "Keep reading." Then, they usually end up saying something like, "Yeah, you're right! I agree with that. I see what you mean."

Read Proverbs 18:13 to see what King Solomon says.

OTHER DEAL-BREAKERS
Not easily categorized

You've Been Incarcerated for a Felony Crime

Men and women expressed distrust in men and women that have been incarcerated; especially for certain crimes. For many women, although it was not listed by any of them in the survey as a deal-breaker, when asked about it, almost all of them responded that this would supersede many of the good qualities.

I then asked them about the men of the Bible or even great men of our time that have turned their lives around., after they had been incarcerated. Some then, changed their answers to something more like, "Well, I would have to know what he has done. OR...I would really have to love him or have already been with him." Others were still adamant about it being a deal-breaker no matter the situation unless the person was totally exonerated and falsely accused.

For many men, being incarcerated was the best thing that ever happened for them. I have spoken with many that it forced them slow down and actually have time to think and get their mind together. For others, it made them worse than they were prior to being incarcerated.

Either way, women and men, when questioned, both said that this could definitely be a deal-breaker.

You've Murdered Someone

Do people change? Yes & No. I believe that people have the potential to change. We just have to make the choice and follow through in order to actually change. Some people believe once a murderer always a murderer. I believe in the healing power of LOVE.

I think that the Creator does forgive and we should as well. It can be a hard thing to do; especially if your family member or friend is the victim.

Knowing that a person has killed another human being can be very hard for someone to get over, and even more difficult to continue to date or marry someone that has murdered someone. So, if this is the issue, this may be the reason that the person you're dating won't marry you.

You've Raped or Sexually Abused Someone

This is another deal-breaker. There are men and women that have been raped, sexually abused and or molested by both men and women. Many of the individuals may never go to jail or receive any kind of punishment for it. However, those that do seem to be marked by society and many are never able to get past that point in their life. The same goes for the victim as well.

I often think that many of the people in our society have faced tragic issues and never receive any

counseling or therapy for the mental damage associated with events such as this. We have a serious decline in the mental health of the average man and woman walking the street.

The sexual desires of many men and women have been heightened largely due to media outpouring of the soft and sometimes not-so-soft SELLING OF SEX. This doesn't excuse anyone to sexually abuse or rape another, but I believe that it has played a role in perpetuating the issue and other issues.

If you've raped, molested, or sexually abused someone, this may be a serious deal-breaker and reason why the person you're dating won't marry you.

You SNORE

I had to put this in the book because when I read this as someone's deal-breaker, I couldn't believe it and laughed almost endlessly. Snoring? I figured that if the young lady that put this as her personal #4 deal-breaker, that there had to be others that wouldn't marry someone because they snored.

I always figured that there was something that could be done about snoring so there was no reason to not marry someone because of this, but maybe I am a little more optimistic about this. If you snore and have a real bad issue with it, be sure to get help as soon as you can. If you are dating someone that you want to marry, the fact that you snore may be the reason they won't marry you. (Laughing. Strange but true!)

WE WANT THE SAME THING, BUT....

Men and women do want the same things. Most of the time, people in general seem to desire the same things in life. The issue seems to be in how we communicate what we desire, or how we expect what we desire to come to us. In our relationships, this seems to hold true.

IMPROPER COMMUNICATION

A little over a year ago I was having a disagreement with my fiancé. This particular disagreement was not the heated "I hate you, you hate me, can't stand you" kind of arguments that couples can sometimes have. It also wasn't the trivial disagreement about the toothpaste, trash, shoes on the floor, didn't clean out the tub, or wash the dishes. It was really a misunderstanding.

She was trying to get me to understand her, and I was trying to get her to understand me. However, neither of us was getting through to the other person. Once we finally stepped away from the situation, I realized the issue was IMPROPER COMMUNICATION. Both of us were trying to be understood by the other, as opposed to both of us trying to understand the other.

I strongly advise all couples and individuals thinking about getting married to take numerous courses on improving their communication skills. Why? According to communication specialists, the least amount of what we say is actually said in WORDS ONLY. The rest of what we communicate is communicated through our tone, volume, facial expressions and body language.

The more skills you have to help you communicate better with your mate, the better. Most people don't have those skills and never take the time to learn or develop them. Therefore, 50% of them don't make it through their marriage, to the "Til Death Do Us Part..." portion of their vows. It would be better to not make a vow than to make it and not work your hardest to keep it.

We also have to take into consideration that according to NLP (Neuro Linguistic Programming) specialists, we all communicate and interpret in 3 major ways; AUDITORY (and Auditory Digital), VISUAL, and KINISTHEITIC. Depending on the primary mode(s) of communication of both you and your partner, you may be having disagreements because the words you use and the words they use, are

causing you to **MISS** what the other person is saying; Therefore, creating constant MISS-understandings.

People communicate differently. This is why you can have two individuals experience a situation and recall the situation totally different. Each individual is interpreting the situation based on their primary modes of communication and interpretation. In order for there to be a more congruent interpretation and ease of communication, both individuals in the relationship should learn to communicate in the other's primary mode of communication. It will be well worth it.

It's worth taking a course and studying communication because 85% of the population primarily communicates from only one of these, only 10% communicate from 2 of these, and only 5% of the population communicates from all 3. Knowing this has helped me personally, but it works better when both people have taken a course and use the skills. If not, the other person may feel that your purpose for trying to reach agreement with them is not genuine and somewhat manipulative.

When we get into a situation of arguing or disagreement, we revert to our primary mode of communication. For me, I actually am one of the 5%. While this is a good thing for me and how I experience life, it can be and has been an issue in past relationships. In most of my relationships, the other person primarily operated in one and maybe two of these modes of communication. This can be difficult because if the right words aren't used and the wrong word is used, it can immediately cause a misunderstanding. When in reality, we are usually trying to communicate the same thing. Sometimes, people need to hear you say certain words in order for their minds to perceive that you understand and that both of you are saying the same thing in a different way.

A Closer Look

One of the most improper ways we communicate is when we tell the other person how they feel or should feel about a situation. The truth is, we can't tell the other person how they feel or should feel. They must tell us, and we can only try our hardest to truly understand what they're saying or how they feel. When you are in a relationship, the way the other person feels in a situation should matter to you if you really love them. If it doesn't, then something is wrong with the LOVE you claim to have for them. To love, you have to care.

"DO NOT TAKE TO HEART EVERYTHING THAT SOMEONE SAYS..."

Many times within our relationships, we become very sensitive about everything the other person says. Someone else that you are not in a relationship of love with, could say the same thing and it not be taken in a negative manner. Why is this? The feelings of love are very sensitive. Because most of us have been hurt in our past relationships, something can be said or done that is similar to past actions, words, or deeds, and still

controls our perception of what is actually being communicated by the other individual. Consequently, if we let it, our past even controls our IMPROPER COMMUNICATION!

If we break the word IMPROPER down into two words, we would have I'M PROPER. And most of the time when we are communicating IMPROPERLY it is because we think that we are the only one in the conversation communicating properly, and that the other person is not!

There is no 'I' in the word PROPER. PROPER COMMUNCIATION INVOLVES "WE." Proper communication is where both individuals involved are **trying to understand the other individual first** and foremost, as opposed to being the only one that is understood. I believe Infinite Intelligence gave us two ears and one mouth for a reason; to do more listening and less talking. When both parties do this, IMPROPER COMMUNICATION will have a hard time trying to win the battle within the relationship.

NOTE FOR THE LADIES: MOST Men stop talking to and stop listening to their woman, if she wants to express how she feels about a situation and never wants to listen to understand what he is thinking or feeling. If he expresses his feelings and you tell him that the way he feels is a lie or that he shouldn't feel a certain way, don't expect for him to want to listen to you or express himself to you in the future. At this point, the damage may have already been done and he usually doesn't desire to talk to you and share his deepest feelings and concerns. And...this is not a good thing for the relationship. Remember, most men, on average use less words per day than you. When he talks, no matter how hard it may be, just listen.

2 Reasons Men & Women Cheat

Men and women want the same thing, but we seem to struggle in our understanding, communication, and desires of how the opposite sex communicates these desires. Every single panel that I have participated in, one of the questions was "Why do men cheat?"

My question is, "Why Do Women Cheat?" Men cheat for the same reason women cheat. They cheat for the same reason anyone cheats at anytime. They cheat because they want to WIN! No one likes to LOSE or the feeling that they are losing, and in most instances, the majority of people will CHEAT (even if it's a little) in order to WIN or to gain an equal footing because they feel like they are being CHEATED.

I also know that some people are not going to be faithful to anyone, and that is just the honest truth. No matter who they date or marry, it's not in them to be faithful. If you want someone to be faithful to you, you have to know if this is an issue for them upfront.

Think about it, many of the most beautiful women in the world, have been cheated on multiple times. It doesn't make a man or woman a bad person if they can't stay faithful. They just may not have the know-how or desire to even be sexually committed to one person; let alone get married and have sex with the same person for the rest of their life. If this is what you desire, do not go for someone that does not display the ability to be faithful.

For both men and women, being unfaithful sexually and emotionally can cause serious issues and emotional pain for all parties involved.

In all the conversations on relationships I participated in over the last 5+ years, everyone that spoke about the subject of cheating gave all kinds of reasons and excuses. In most cases, they expressed the hurt and pain that came from it. Behind everything that everyone was saying, I heard two things that were very consistent in all that was being said; lack of Appreciation & Attention.

Both men and women want APPRECIATION and ATTENTION. We just seem to have a different order of importance when it comes to these two relationship needs.

A WOMAN'S HEIARCHY

ATTENTION

APPRECIATION

A woman wants ATTENTION first and APPRECIATION second. A woman wants to know that you notice her. She wants you to pay attention to her. She wants to know that you noticed that she changed her hair, or that she painted her nails. She wants you to notice if she lost a few pounds or beautified the premises, etc. She wants your attention.

This is why she instinctively may wait until you're preoccupied with watching the game or on an important call before she comes and interrupts you with something that she could have told you hours ago. The funny part about a woman is that sometimes when you give her too much attention; it has the potential of backfiring to the point that she may lose interest. But if you don't pay her enough attention, she will begin to seek it elsewhere.

This is why even wealthy men may be cheated on by their mate because while they can PAY FOR ANYTHING SHE DESIRES, they often feel they CAN'T AFFORD TO PAY HER SOME ATTENTION.

A MAN NEEDS...

A man needs attention as well, but not near as much as he NEEDS APPRECIATION. Women often get this part twisted because they are thinking from their own minds and what they would desire. A man needs to hear and know that you appreciate him more than you need his attention.

<u>A MAN'S HEIARCHY</u>

APPRECIATION

ATTENTION

Knowing that you appreciate the fact that he takes out the garbage, helps around the house, rubbed your feet, tried to cook, or anything else, makes him feel good and actually gets you the thing that you want from him, ATTENTION and more help, money, participation, etc.

The more you APPRECIATE him, the more he ATTENDS to you and your wants, needs, and desires. A man goes to work, makes money, and takes care of his family to be appreciated at the end of each day by his children, but even more so by his woman. The women that understand and practice this, rarely have a problem keeping a man.

I told this to one woman and she said, "I am not his mother. He doesn't need to be appreciated and praised for that. That is what he is supposed to do. He's a man." I laughed because when I asked her, "Really? Well, what are you supposed to do if you're not supposed to do this?" She didn't respond.

It seems to be easy to know that to motivate your man to the highest of heights that he could achieve, your main focus would need to be to make him feel appreciated, and in turn, he would give you the attention that you desire; which in turn would make you feel appreciated and would cause you to give him attention.

Both parties would be satisfied; giving & receiving what they desire. A woman that knows this possesses much POWER. Most that do know and use this power do not use it to benefit themselves and the rest of the world because few have been taught how and why to do so. Let's take a closer look.

The 3 C's Men Must Know in Order to Marry You...

Cost. A man looks at most things in Assets and Liabilities. And since he does, let's use real estate for our example. An asset adds value or gain to your bottom line. Liabilities cost you and take away from your bottom line.

In a buyer's market, for the man that has not found the house that he wants, he will continue to rent. He may even do a month to month lease so that he

won't have a long-term commitment.

A man that is actively looking for a house because he is tired of renting, will get preapproved, secure an agent, know what he is looking for, know his budget, the value of the house, the problems, if it is not a new house what needs to be improved, and if it will add value to his life or be a headache and a liability.

He must know the COST. Not the monthly payment, but the total cost to maintain it. He looks at you the same way. If your maintenance cost is too much for him, he will probably not marry you. If he has to invest too much time, effort, energy, money, to get you and maintain you, he will probably rethink the decision and have serious apprehensions concerning you and marriage. This is why there are plenty of beautiful women that are single. It's not because they want to be (As many of them will openly say) it's because they are a liability, and THE JUICE IS NOT WORTH THE SQUEEZE.

When it's a BUYER'S MARKET as it is currently, many people are choosing to rent. Many men are the same way during periods where there are many more available women than there are in comparison to available and eligible men.

Care. A man must know that you CARE about him as a person. He needs to know that you care about how he feels and what he has to say. He needs to know that you care about him for who he is and where he is in life, and not what he has and/or doesn't have.

He needs to know that you care about his well being. He needs to know that you will care for him when and/or if that time actually comes; such as sickness or health issues.

Many men that most would consider to be MARRIAGE MATERIAL say, "Unless they have children, women now-a-days don't care about anyone but themselves." Others say, "The average woman is looking for a meal ticket or a come up. They act as if they care, but let a small storm or cold breeze blow through and watch how they change or blow with the wind."

These men also feel that as long as things are good, the woman is with you. As long as you are saying all the right things and letting them throw fits but never getting upset, they are with you. However, if a time comes where you aren't this perfect prince, they are second guessing things and you become the villain. No matter how many times they have cussed you out, fussed, nagged, or even hit you, if you show any signs of anger, they all of the sudden don't trust you. Many feel that they are the only one in relationships that are supposed to show any emotions. This is unrealistic and not a fair assessment of the male gender.

Contrary to popular belief, men have feelings, express their emotions in multiple ways other than shutting down, and can be quite sensitive. Remember, there are both male & female genes in the male (XY). You have to care about how he feels if you want him to be concerned with how you feel. He may act as if he cares, but actually doesn't if he feels you don't care. He

will be agreeable with you only for the sake of keeping the peace, but will not be genuinely happy because he is not able to be himself within the relationship.

Commitment. A man needs to know that you are committed to him. When I say committed I mean; committed to him and not just to the relationship. A man can feel when a woman is committed to the relationship and not to him. What do I mean? Many times a woman can become committed to the 'CHARTER BUS' that we spoke of earlier.

She will be in the relationship, but even the relationship seems to be about everyone and everything else in her life and not about her or the guy she is dating. She wants to be able to tell her friends about his new job or promotion, new car, trip he is planning to take her on, or how much money he's making, show off her ring, gift that he just bought her, where he took her out to eat, and so on and so on. It always seems to be about including everyone and everything else in the equation of "WE."

Commitment to a man looks like this:

YOU+ME = WE

Commitment to a woman looks more like this:

YOU + ME / (My mother + best friend + Job + close friends + pet + children) = US

As one female respondent wrote as one of her TOP 5 Deal-Breakers: ***"I can't marry a man if my family does not mesh well with the personality of the significant other. I need harmony."***

Sunday, September 30, 2012 3:35:16 AM

She wants to be able to IMPRESS or IMPRESS UPON these individuals that her life is good, and that she loves them and that they are just as important as this man if not more important. A man is usually not concerned with what they think. He is not concerned about them knowing how much money he makes, what kind of car he drives, where he stays, or what he does for a living. A man that is seriously committed to you is concerned about you being committed to him and not to this idea of a relationship that you may want to portray. He is concerned about LOVING YOU.

You are his family and he is your family. You two are to start your own family. You BOTH must leave your mother and father and cleave to one another. When a man loves, he really loves. He gives you his heart. If he has had his heart broken before, he will not be as eager in most cases to fall in love again.

He doesn't want to be that vulnerable again. He needs to know that you are committed to his vision. It's easy to be committed to what appears to be already in place, but not as easy to be committed to something that is in its beginning stages or only in the mind of another.

The average man has his vision that he has been dreaming about, working towards, and thinking about that must be committed to by himself and his mate in most cases. Even if she is not actively committed to it, she must be committed to motivating him towards the achievement of his end result. If he is a man of CHARACTER & VISION, he will probably not marry you if you are not committed to him.

Never Date Someone You Wouldn't Marry

The powerful statement *"Never date someone you wouldn't marry..."* came to me in my 11th grade English class. The students in this particular class were a little snobby upper middle class and what most people would consider to be "well-off." Many times, these students would tease the teacher to try and get her to cry. She could be rather emotional and on this particular day she actually started crying. Finally, after they achieved their goal of making her cry, one of the students asked her what was wrong. Once she gained her composure she said, ***"Never date someone you wouldn't marry because you just might fall in love with them."***

As a 16 year old young man, I must say that this was as profound to me then as it is right now. It made me think. The statement by itself has probably saved thousands of people heartache that they otherwise would have had to experience.

You see, when you fall in love with someone that you know you wouldn't marry, you may end up negatively affecting multiple lives of other individuals and your own. You may also waste a lot of years, and a lot of time; the whole time knowing that this person is someone that you absolutely would not marry.

Think about this...You wouldn't go to McDonald's ® to order Fettuccini Alfredo. You would go to Olive Garden® or some other Italian restaurant for this dish and to a burger place if you wanted a burger. If you do, you're basically trying to get the cook to make what is not on the menu, and also a dish that they don't have the ingredients for. They would look at you crazy if you did this at either restaurant. Many times we do this same thing in relationships. We're trying to get a big juicy burger, fries, and a shake from an Italian restaurant that doesn't serve it. Or, we may be trying to get Fettucini Alfredo from a burger joint that doesn't have the ingredients. The sooner you figure out whether or not what you're looking for is on the menu, the better for all parties involved because...

Time is the one thing you can't get back!

As the background lyrics in Lee Ann Womack's classic hit song, *I Hope You Dance* say, *"Time is a wheel in constant motion always rolling us along. Tell me who wants to look back on their years and wonder where those years have gone."* The years go by so fast. Appreciate each and every day.

ADDICTED to the FEELING

Why do people do this you might ask? The feeling of falling in love is almost like a drug. During the earliest stages of dating and falling in love, up to about 18 months (sometimes less), the brain releases an increased amount of many of the same 'feel good' chemicals that it releases during illicit drug use. After this time period, what happens is that the animal attraction or intense desire usually starts to fade because the chemicals being released also slow down. This is the reason why many people keep going from relationship to relationship thinking that it's going to be different.

People become addicted to the feeling of fun and excitement, intense sex, and a natural high that happens during the early stages of dating because of these increased release of chemicals in the brain. Usually, once the release of these chemicals in the brain slow down, the test of love really kicks in. This is why I believe it is referred to as 'FALLING IN LOVE.' You literally feel like you are very vulnerable and falling into this place that you don't know where, in hopes that the 'FEELING OF FALLING' will never end. But...you're also hoping that when you reach the ground, there will be someone there to catch you.

Many in today's society actively choose not to fall and just enjoy the short periods of dating for 6 months, a year, 14 months, or however long it takes for the chemicals to wear off or the feeling to fade. Then, one day when they look up and time has just passed; it's 5, 6, 7, or 10 years later, and you have now developed a pattern. You've become addicted to the FEELING OF FALLING IN LOVE, but still have NO LOVE.

The pattern may be even worse for you. You may not even be capable of receiving love by this time let alone giving it. Love becomes only an idea to you. You may believe in it for others, but not something that you see as real for your own life. False fantasies of what love should be remain in the mind because no one ever really made it clear to you what LOVE is really all about.

At this point, as opposed to operating from the spirit of LOVE where you LOVE WITHOUT LIMITS (Diagram 1); you now have a LEARNED BEHAVIOR style of loving. You learn to give a pseudo LOVE (Diagram 2).

More detail on this and further explanation of the diagrams on the next page, are in my Amazon.com bestselling book, The Love Triangle: How to Heal from a Broken Heart (Hurt, Shame Bitterness, & Betrayal).

Diagram 1

Diagram 2

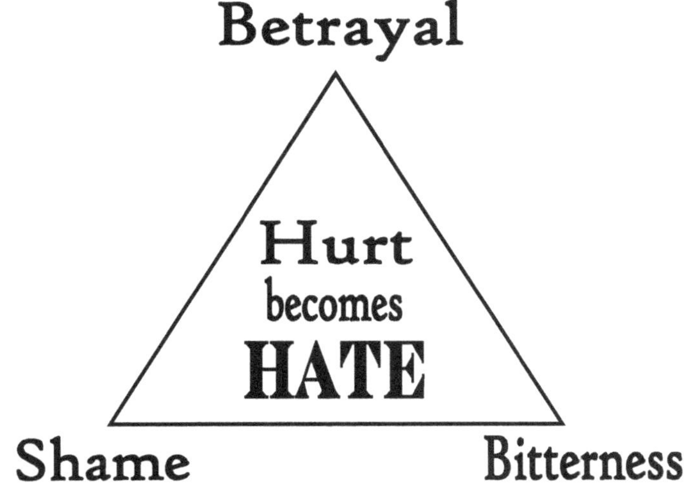

All of this may be the reason why most religions advise individuals to wait until they're married before having sex. Not doing so has the potential to create 'collateral damage; especially for a woman. Why? As a woman, you usually have to make a mental decision, emotional decision, and a physical decision before ever having sex with a man.

Sometimes you only make the mental and the physical decision in hopes of avoiding the emotional decision to have sex with the man; thinking you'll save yourself from getting attached and keeping it just physical. In most cases, when this happens, the emotional decision is made by default, or the fight against become emotionally attached begins to happen. This makes you, in most cases, twice as vulnerable in the situation as the man.

As a woman, no one has to tell you to love. It is a very natural thing for you to do. You are naturally a lover. Anything opposite of love that you display is a LEARNED BEHAVIOR. Men first experience LOVE from their mothers. Therefore, when a man doesn't LOVE, it too is a LEARNED BEHAVIOR. A man's natural propensity is to protect. No one has to tell a young boy to protect his sisters or younger siblings. It is natural within him. Anything opposite of this is A LEARNED BEHAVIOR.

When a man loves, remember, he gives you his heart. If a man is not a loving man, he is a man whose heart has been hurt and sometimes totally destroyed. So, if you're truly loving a man and not feeling the love from him in return, he may be doing the other thing

that is natural to him; TRYING TO PROTECT. And what he is trying to protect, even at the expense of hurting you, is his own heart.

Because we have learned many behaviors that are not natural to us, we MUST remember to GIVE WHAT WE WANT TO RECEIVE. In order to do this, you must FIRST know what you want.

Just remember, *Love is patient, love is kind. It does not envy, it does not boast, it is not proud. It does not dishonor others, it is not self-seeking, it is not easily angered, and it keeps no record of wrongs. Love does not delight in evil but rejoices with the truth. It always protects, always trusts, always hopes, and always perseveres.*

REVIEW

Men see relationships as a __________ or __________.

Women see relationships as a ____________________.

Define Marriage Material:

____

____

____

Define Chase vs. Pursue: _______________________

____

____

Would you honestly define yourself as more of a giver or a receiver? ______________________________.
Please explain why?: ___________________________

____

____

A woman brings ____________& ____________ to a man's mind.

It is ______ ______ for man to be ______________.

<u>List YOUR TOP 3 DEAL-BREAKERS:</u>

1. ____
2. ____
3. ____

SPIRITUAL REASONS

I strongly believe that we are spiritual beings having a physical experience. I have believed this since I was a little boy. No one had to tell me this. It has always been something that I just innately understood. It had nothing to do with the church I went to or what religion my ancestors were; I just knew that I was more than the flesh I looked at in the mirror everyday and so was everyone else.

In my attempt to bridge as many gaps as I can in the religious ideologies of many, I want to say that it all boils down to LOVE. Every major religion on the earth believes in one thing for sure; LOVE. Love is the uniting factor. It is the one thing that has no gender, race, religion, color, or economic background.

In America, and in most countries around the world, vows are taken in front of a clergy or judge. In the ceremony, this person unites the man and woman under the laws of the land and God.

However, no matter the vows, secular or religious, marriage in today's time seems to be less and less about the spiritual union and more about things that don't matter.

Spirituality is a central piece of who we are as individuals and collectively. We are definitely spiritual beings having a spiritual experience. We are not our religion. However, many people confuse religion and spirituality. Marriage is and should be a spiritual connection.

#1 – You're not a believer in God, Allah, Jehovah, Yahweh or a Supreme Source or Creator of All. The belief of one God or Source from which all things originate predates all known organized religions. While the majority of the people in the world believe in some sort of original source or creator, there are those that do not. If you are one of those that don't, do not be surprised if this is the reason that the person may not marry you.

#2 – You have a different religion. Many times people mistake God for religion. I then ask them "What is God's Religion?" Some will try and answer the question, but most do not because who are we to say what Religion God has? The majority of the people will

say what I know to be true, "He doesn't have one!" Who has all the truth that was ever revealed upon the earth in all of the millions of years that there has ever been an earth?

Which person or religion has the exact date and time of everything that has ever happened? Not one person. Not one religion. I am all for people believing how they want to believe. However, many people use this as a reason not to marry someone or to marry them. While this may be the reason you won't marry a man or woman, understand that most of the time people change and evolve throughout their life. Therefore, their religion and/or how they understand their religion usually do as well.

Muhammad Ali said, *"If a man thinks the same at 50 as he did when he was 20, he has wasted 30 years of his life."*

#3 – You don't practice what you say you believe. For some people this is a big deal. For me, it is because it doesn't show congruency. I don't expect anyone to be perfect, but a certain effort towards what you say you follow should be there. I strongly and firmly believe as I stated earlier that the basis of all major religions is LOVE. So, when I see people that claim to believe in Judaism, Christianity, Islam, Buddhism, Hinduism, or any religion of the likes of these, I am expecting to see a person working to display love towards their fellowman. The only issue in our world today is that there seems to be less love towards one another. Love is looked at as a sign of weakness if you actually love in our generation.

Many women and men that took the survey for this book mentioned this as a deal breaker. Even though the person they were dating may have gone to the same church, mosque, or synagogue they didn't feel that the person was dedicated to what they say they believe. Therefore, they chose not to marry the person.

#4 – I don't understand what you believe or I don't agree. This is a tricky one because what goes into the mind first is usually what the mind thinks is right; even if it isn't. Sometimes, in different religions, it's not so much that one thing is not true and another is, but rather based on the information provided one seems to be right over the other. When this happens and the other person has no knowledge of it and uses their book or their information as more credible than that of another's information, confusion and misunderstanding can easily take precedence. **Look for commonality as opposed to differences.**

#5 – You don't pay tithes or give to others for spiritual/community betterment. Some may or may not agree with this, but I think that money is a very spiritual thing. Most people have been taught that money is not good or that having a lot of it isn't good. I know because at one point in my life I viewed it as such.

I was 20 years old and looked at the $10/hour I was making as a lot of money. I thought for the work I was doing versus the pay I was receiving, as robbery of the US taxpayers. Boy, have I grown since then.

However, I have always believed in giving. At times, I would give until I had given out more than I

had for myself on some occasions. While this may have been the philanthropic thing to do, paying a tithe or a set amount would have been much more spiritual than giving as in a sacrificial manner.

Contrary to popular belief, the majority of wealthy people are givers that believe in the principle of tithing and giving.

In my own life, "Giving has been one of the most important practices that I have developed since I was a child. It has given me what I like to call FAVOR!" Being able to give is a gift within itself. Giving opens the door for you to receive even more than what you give.

Sexual Reasons

Sex is a language that all people of the earth understand. It is the one language other than music and love that transcends gender, age, race, religion and socioeconomic background. It is the process through which life is continued. Sex is the act that makes us co-creators with Infinite Intelligence.

According to many, sex is the most powerful stimuli or motivating force in the Universe. It's benefits are so powerful, that it can literally heal a person.

#1 – You have an STD. While I was out one night selling my books at a then very popular night club in Dallas, I met a young man that bought one of my books. We spoke briefly. As he was talking to me, I felt that he wanted to tell me a few things other than the surface conversation that we were having.

I often sense what's going on with people more than I knew I actually did. This particular case was one of those. As I kept talking to the young man he mentioned his young child. I then asked him about his child's mother and their relationship. He told me that they had broken up after the child was born. He said that he loved and didn't want her to leave, but that is the way it had worked out. I then asked him about the possibility of them getting back together. He said, "I would have loved to get back with her, but while we were away, she slept with someone else." I said, "I understand that, but you love her and your child, right?" He said, "Yes! But she got an STD from one of the guys she was with. I tried to get over it and get passed it, but I just couldn't. For my own health and safety, I just couldn't get back with her."

This was a very important meeting and conversation. Sometimes, we think that the grass is greener. The grass is greener where you pull up the weeds, water it, and fertilize it. As the old people used to say, "Don't jump out of the frying pan into the fire!" This is exactly what this young lady did.

As a woman, you are the receivers of sex. Man is the giver. I'll say again, "A man can't have consensual sex with you unless YOU open YOUR legs." It is easier for a woman to get a sexually transmitted disease or infection because she is the receiver. The responsibility to protect yourself sexually is not the responsibility of the other person...it is your responsibility.

For more on this, visit the Centers for Disease Control's website at www.cdc.org.

#2 – Too Many Partners. Years ago, while I was in my men's class, one of the brother's said, "I wish I had not had sex with so many women before I got married because it has made it harder for me to stay faithful to my wife." Hearing this from a man that was a faithful husband, father, and standard in the community was eye opening and awakening.

They say, "A woman has to kiss a lot of frogs in order to find her prince." This is quite funny because in the kissing of the frogs, it often goes a little further than just kissing. So, by the time she is 30 years old, not married, and has no children, she has created a pattern. She has created a pattern of leaving a relationship or being left. When her deepest desire is usually to be with a man that will love her and that she can love in return. While she may believe that this can happen, the more men she has been with the more men she compares each new man with. Meaning, each new guy is not starting out in the relationship on a clean slate no matter how much he thinks he is.

#3 – You've cheated or been sexually unfaithfully. If a man or woman cheats in the relationship, it is very easy to make the decision not to marry them. In most cases, if a person will cheat before marrying you, they will do the same thing in marriage. If you have done this, you have put a BIG HOLE in the blanket of trust. Therefore, this may be the reason that the person you want to marry you will not marry you.

#4 – You had sex with someone I know, am related to or someone that I am friends with. For some people this is not a reason to not marry a person. For others, it is like breaking the law or the rules of engagement in war. I could see how it could mentally be an issue for the person using this as their reason to not marry. I would say that this is a valid reason not to marry; especially if children were produced from the situation. It can definitely cause a whole lot of confusion.

#5 – Sex has not been great with you. This particular reason was listed multiple times on my survey of the TOP 5 Deal breakers. Both men and women listed this as a reason.

Many years ago in our society and around the world, this may not have been as big of an issue because there was less promiscuity. Therefore, people did not know what they had or had not sexually experienced. However, in the time we live today, you have the largest new cases of HIV coming from the ages of 13-29 years of age. You have 30 million people worldwide with HIV/AIDS. Therefore, people are HAVING SEX, and individuals are having sex younger and younger.

So, most women and men by the time they are married or find someone to get married to, they are sexually comparing the person to someone else. This leads me to the next reason.

#6 – You don't want to wait until marriage before having sex, or you want to wait until marriage before having sex. Multiple women that I know, even those that consider themselves to be believers in monotheistic religions (all of which are against premarital sex), have said these words to me, "I HAVE TO TEST DRIVE BEFORE I BUY!" Even if they are willing to wait or trying to be celibate, they will want to have foreplay, touch and feel, etc.

I believe most men would wait, but it is not the popular thing to do now-a-days amongst women. So, there is no way for us to be expected to wait when the majority of the women in our society are not concerned with waiting. This makes it very easy for us when one woman won't have sex with us, to still get sex because another female will.

Now, there are also many women and some men that will not have sex before marriage for different reasons. Whatever the reason may be, the fact that you do want to have sex and not respect their desire not to do so, may be the very reason why the person does not want to marry you. This quality should be a very pleasing quality for both a man and a woman, and a reason that should make you want to marry the person even more. It shows self control; especially for a man to actively choose to abstain from sex.

I think that LOVE is better than SEX. I will be the first to say that SEX is a very wonderful and powerful thing. Conversely, it is a much better experience when LOVE is present between two people versus LUST.

As the R&B singer Trey Songz sings in one of his songs, "I've been out here in the streets and I've learned...SEX AIN'T BETTER THAN LOVE."
It can be very easy to confuse SEX with LOVE.

As I was writing in a previous chapter, about the chemicals being released during those first 18 months, the other part of this is even better. The period that happens after this is where LOVE can actually be developed. According to multiple research studies, couples that have been with the same partner for long periods of time are said to have the most satisfying sex lives; in comparison to those that are newly married, dating, engaged, etc.

#7 – You like to use sex as a means of control.
No man or woman really likes to be controlled or feel as if they are being controlled. I personally know that as a man, when a woman tries to use sex as a means of control, it only works for a period of time before the man gets tired and decides to go elsewhere. This is an okay thing to do when there is a set time and date or specific goal given.

A man can usually wait if and when he knows the end to that which he is waiting on. When there is just an uncertainty as a way of controlling him or the situation, you will have to use the same tactic each time you want to control a situation; therefore, making it less and less effective each time.

If the man or woman is being faithful, it is easier for them just to find someone else as opposed to being misused on the basis of sex in order for the other

person to get what they desire in the situation.

#8 – You've gone too far sexually with others. I personally believe that sex is one of the most spiritual acts if not the most spiritual act that we perform. When you enter a woman or allow a man to enter your body, you are taking upon the essence of them and all before them. You take on their energy. Energy is neither created nor destroyed. Therefore, you must be very careful who you have sex with.

Some things that people partake in sexually are not natural. I won't go into any detail, but certain places and things are not and have not been made for sexual pleasure.

When you have sex with someone you know them in a way that even their own mother or father (in the majority of cases) will never know them.

If a person has apprehensions about your sexual experiences and uses this as the reason why they don't want to marry you, I hope you will understand. They may not tell you this, but for many men and women, this can be a problem.

#9 – You've had sex with the same gender, and still have the tendencies. Okay, this is a touchy subject. I am putting this in the book because it is a real issue that many women today may have to face. Women may be approached by a man that has had sex in the past with men, but consider themselves as heterosexual. This is what is known as the "Down Low" and has posed a threat to the longevity of life for women and African-American women in particular.

I was watching a reality television show I had never seen before. The show was about a man that was married to a woman; he said he was heterosexual, worked as a homosexual porn actor that actually had sex with other men. This was very confusing and I could see the strain that it caused on the wife. I could see the years of life that this lifestyle had drained from her. It was not a good look. I am all for people being free to make their own decisions and do what they want to do. However, I don't believe that you should bring other people into a situation or decision that you make that could be detrimental to them in multiple ways.

The point is this, if you have had sex with another man and you still wish to do so, don't marry a woman that is not cool with this. Don't marry him or her and then spring this on them years down the line, when you knew upfront this was the lifestyle you wanted to live. Why? You are sending her through some things that she doesn't have to go through.

If a man or woman doesn't want to marry you for this reason, this is a valid reason and you should understand.

EMOTIONAL REASONS

#1 – You're inability to express love or express it in the language that I understand. I have never read Gary Chapman's book, The Five Love Languages, but from working within the industry, I am familiar with the concept. According to everyone I know that has, I understand being able to speak the other person's love language will help improve the relationship. And... I definitely understand most people *do not define love the same way that their partner defines it*. Many times, especially when it comes to emotions, it seems as if we are not only from two different planets, but now-a -days, it seems as if we are from two different galaxies.

If you plan on being married, it would be a great idea to read as much as you can on the subject and take as many premarital courses that you can. I believe that it will be well worth the investment.

#2 – You're too unhappy too often. In order to be happy you have to be happy. For some reason, this seems to be a hard thing for people to do. This was a reason that me and many other men expressed as something that we could not deal with. A man likes to be able to know that he is with a happy woman prior to getting engaged and definitely before getting married.

A happy woman makes a happy home. So, if there is an unhappy woman in the household the husband will more than likely be unhappy, and so will the children and everyone else.

A woman that is happy can more easily create a happy home even if the man has made the household a little unhappy. A woman that loves is an extremely powerful person, and there is nothing that can withstand love. Love conquers all. This is the day that the Lord has made, I shall rejoice and be glad in it.

#3 – You have a Negative attitude about life, self, and others. Some people may not be unhappy all the time, but they seem to have a very negative attitude about life and the world in general. They seem to doubt everything. They seem to critique everything and everybody. They find fault all around them in everyone else except themselves. As the great Zig Ziglar says, "They have developed a case of stinking thinking!"

This type of person can easily poison the relationship and damage the self-esteem of their partner. The long-term effects from being in a relationship such as this are sometimes irreversible; especially concerning your emotional well being.

#4 – You worry too much about things that don't matter. It's amazing how most of what we worry about never happens. A person that is constantly stressing about toothpaste, making the bed, or which way that tissue was supposed to be placed on the holder, needs to take a chill pill. Life is too short!

Worry creates stress and tension, which produces sickness and disease. When we're tense we are not relaxed. Most people that are not relaxed or happy, are usually difficult to deal with. No one wants to constantly have to deal with an irritable individual. Their worry and stress then becomes your problem. This usually causes you undue and unneeded stress. You have your own stress to handle.

A man or woman cannot function properly when the person or persons around them are constantly worrying about things and situations that they cannot control; and don't matter in the overall scheme of things.

#5 – You are angry too often for no apparent reason. After a person becomes too tense too often and does not have a way to release this tension, it will usually end up being expressed through frustration, irritability, and ultimately anger. Anger is a strong emotion that is expressed by different people in different ways. Some people are not able to handle too much stress for too long and will break or snap. This breaking or snapping moment seems to be easily triggered in some people and less in others. Depending on the tolerance level of the individual, their breaking point will have much to do with their own personal history or the amount of stress on the body and mind at that time. Certain things for certain people are a DO NOT CROSS THIS LINE type of situation. I would not ever test someone that has told you what LINES TO NOT CROSS with them.

I may not be politically correct with this, but I don't think a woman should hit a man just as much as I don't think that a man should hit a woman. Most men are physically stronger than women. The average woman that is 150 pounds is more than likely not as strong as the average man that is 150 pounds. This is one of those actual and factual differences that I spoke of in the first chapter. With this being said, I would advise a woman to not hit a man because doing so may have put you in a DO NOT CROSS THIS LINE situation with this man, which you more than likely will not win.

Being hit by a man or a woman doesn't feel good. I always put it to women like this, DO NOT GET INTO A VERBAL BATTLE WITH A MAN because in most cases he will LOSE; not all but most! He knows he will most likely lose; this is why he is usually not as vocal as you are. Remember, you use on average 10,000 – 15,000 more words per day than he does. Therefore, he is fighting a losing battle before the fight even starts. Innately knowing this, in most cases, he will not pick a verbal fight with you. However, I tell women this all the time, YOUR STRENGTH IS IN THE HIDING OF YOUR POWER. You don't go around flexing your muscles and bullying a man just because you can. It would equate to the same as him knowing that he is physically stronger than you walking around hitting you every time he gets ready.

You may be thinking, "No it's not the same thing." Trust me...to a man...it is! This is why he will either walk away and never return, or eventually end up trying to defend himself the way he knows how; physically.

If you are a person that gets ANGRY too often for no apparent reason, THIS MAY BE THE REASON, man or woman, why the other person won't marry you.

#6 – You have an extreme amount of fear(s). Fear is even worse than worry. FEAR is seriously FALSE EVIDENCE APPEARING REAL. Fear is a step up from worry. People that have seriously feared things usually develop what is called a PHOBIA of some kind. Most phobias are not healthy.

I believe that we only have two fears as babies; The Fear of Falling and the Fear of Loud Noises. I have observed multiple babies and children and now my own, and noticed that every other fear is a learned behavior. Even within me, the fears that I have are based on situations that happened that caused pain of some kind or extreme stress that I want to avoid. Over the years, I have constantly challenged myself to overcome the fears that I developed in the younger years of my life.

A person with extreme fears can be so fearful of a certain situation that they can actually go into panic and have a panic attack or heart attack. My mother's old beautician actually died from being in an MRI because she was so scared of being closed in.

The mind is a powerful. The emotion of FEAR in MOST cases is more detrimental than it is helpful. If you are a person with EXTREME FEAR, especially if for no apparent reason, THIS MAY BE THE REASON WHY the other person WON'T MARRY YOU.

#7 – Still in love with someone else. Marrying or choosing to marry someone that is still in love with someone else is not a wise thing to do. Both men and women have the ability to be in a relationship with one person, but still be in love with someone else. If the person you want to marry is feeling apprehensive about marrying you, this could definitely be the reason WHY they may NOT MARRY YOU.

Always properly heal your heart before moving on to the next relationship. Why? Because...

Hurt people Hurt People.

If the person you're dating doesn't want to marry you, it may be because you are still in love with someone else.

#8 – Emotionally inconsistent aka Emotional Roller Coaster. A roller coaster is a fun ride once or maybe twice, but after being on the ride any longer than that you will become sick.

Many men have stated that many women that they deal with have emotional inconsistencies or roller coasters, that suck you in and then you begin to become like them. By the time you have realized it, it's too late because it is as if you have been manipulated to the point of confusion and even bitterness.

#9 – Blame everyone else for your emotional instability. Many people that have issues with emotional instability rarely take responsibility for their participation in a situation. Everything that has happened in their life that was not good was somehow not their doing. It is always someone else's fault. If someone cussed them out, it's the other person's fault. If they hit someone and get hit back it's somehow the other person's fault.

If you can't take responsibility for your own emotional instability, this may be the reason the person you're dating won't marry you.

10

Physical Reasons

We live in a world where the physical reality is the only reality to most people. If they can't see it or touch it, it's not real. If they can see it, they usually believe it, even if it is not what it actually appears to be. One of my favorite quotes came from the movie, "The Karate Kid." The quote was, "You see only with your eyes, therefore you are easily fooled."

#1 - The Five Second Rule. One night while I was out promoting my book, 99 Questions, I met a young lady that is now my friend. Her name is Sakenia. She is an upwardly mobile registered nurse that is very sweet and community minded. A great catch.

As I was out promoting, she stopped immediately as soon as she saw me with the book. I didn't know what was going on. With excitement she said, "I have been trying to find this book after hearing you talk about it on the radio." She was really excited to meet me. Of course, I was excited to meet her too. I am always excited to meet people that I don't know that are excited to meet me, and know about me prior to actually meeting me. She bought the book, and asked me about other books that I may have had coming out.

As we talked more, she began to ask me about relationships & marriage. She asked, Why is it so difficult to get a man to actually want to marry a woman now-a-days." I told her as I tell a lot of women, "I am sure that if you're 30 years of age or older you have had a man that has wanted to marry you, that would have actually been good to you." She replied, "I haven't!" I told her, "Yes you have!" She said, "No I... you know what...you're right...I HAVE! But there is no way I could marry this man." I asked her "Why not?" She laughed and then said, "I have this rule...The 5-second Rule." Now of course I asked her, "What is the 5 -second rule?" She replied, "If I can't look at a man for more than 5 seconds without thinking, DAMN HE's UGLY! I CAN'T BE WITH HIM!" I couldn't do anything but laugh.

I then told her, "When I complete my book, *This Is Why I Won't Marry You*, I will include this story in the book." Thanks Sakenia.

If you are not physically attractive to the person that you want to marry you, they may not marry you. I can see where Sakenia is coming from. She definitely knew what she didn't want. She had some guidelines. They weren't too bad. She was even willing to be with

someone that wasn't her ideal guy he just had to be able to pass her 5-Second Rule. This particular guy was only one second shy of being able to date and marry her. She saw all the good in him in other ways, but one of her deal-breakers was not being able to pass the 5-Second Rule.

#2 – Too Short (Women). Most of the time, women have height requirements. Very few women that I've met, don't have some sort of height requirement. I'm 6'1" and women shorter than me have called me short. I laugh because these same women are usually 5'3" – 5'9" without heals. They put heels on and forget their real height. If you're 5'2" and date a guy that is 5'7" I don't think that should be an issue. Even if you're 5'10" and date a guy 6'0" if you love him and he loves you, I don't think you should miss out on a good mate for marriage. Many women pass over good men because they aren't tall enough.

#3 – Too Tall (Men). Sometimes, men can be intimidated by a woman taller than them. Some men don't care. However, in our society, if you're a tall woman or a short man, you can be picked on and ridiculed. As stated above, many times a man may not even approach a woman because of her height.

To the men reading this book, approach her anyway and remind her that she has on heels. Then proceed forth with the conversation. Now, if you are in a relationship with her, try your best not to ever make this an issue. If she is in a relationship with you, she more than likely has accepted this as an okay situation and has gotten past it.

Don't let this stop you from asking her to marry you if you really love her.

If the person you're dating won't marry you, the fact that you're too tall may be the reason.

#4 – Your Weight. Again, we live in a society that places a lot on physical appearance and looks. Your weight may be a deciding factor for a man or woman to not marry you. Jokes have been made by the women that I have been in serious relationships with concerning my weight. I don't know how much of a deciding factor this would have been for marriage, but they definitely ridiculed me for being slim. Some men and women will not marry someone that is too slim or skinny. Thank God I am secure about my weight and who I am.

One young lady that I dated when I first started this book had a serious issue with her self-image and perception of her weight. I thought she looked great, and was quite attractive. This was an issue for her because she didn't see herself as such. The high school she went to was a little preppy, and if you had any kind of curves, you were considered fat. So, in her mind she was fat because her body type was not the status quo.

So, being slim or not so slim can be an issue for the person you are dating. However, if they are dating you and love you, your weight is probably more of an issue for you than it is for them.

#5 – Physically let your appearance go lacking. You must be able to keep yourself maintained. Sometimes, it's not an easy thing to do; especially depending on the circumstances in your life. Appearance is important. If you want a person to marry you, and you have been dating them for a while, you can't get lazy with your physical upkeep.

Your physical upkeep can be a task all of its own, but it is a very important task if you desire to be married. Why? What goes through the other person's mind is, "Can I look at this person everyday for the rest of my life." If your physical appearance is not neat and clean, and you are not groomed well on a regular basis, the person you are dating may begin to become less and less attracted to you. IF this is the case, they may begin to have doubts about marrying you.

#6 – Physical conditions I can't get past. This was one piece that I didn't necessarily want to put into the book, but in order to stay true to what people have said their reasons for not marrying someone was, it was very important to do so.

Some physical issues that people have they are born with; others have physical conditions that happened from different situations in life. Either way, the person is not their physical condition.

However, if you have a certain physical condition, this may be the reason the person you're dating won't marry you.

Health Reasons

#1 – You Smoke, Drink, Do drugs (And have no desire or making effort to quit). I am all for people doing what they want to do with their life as long as it does not negatively affect others. There are certain things that negatively affect others as well as the individual that chooses to do the act. Second hand smoke is worse than first hand smoke. Therefore, the person that smokes cigarettes around other people that don't smoke is actually rather selfish. Getting drunk on a regular basis has numerous negative outcomes that may affect other people as well as the person that gets drunk. History has shown has that over a period of time, the use of drugs and alcohol has rarely ever ended well for the users and/or those closest to them.

Addictions of all kind can be detrimental, and difficult to rid yourself of the addiction. If you are in love with someone that's someone that suffers with an addiction, please encourage them to seek professional help. It is important for you and for them that they receive freedom from their addiction. There's no way you can say that you love them if you're not willing to help them seek professional help. There's also no way that they can really love themselves if they are not willing to cure their addiction.

If the person you're dating does not want to marry you, the fact that you smoke, drink, do drugs, and are not actively trying to quit may be the reason they will not marry you.

#2 – You don't exercise. Exercise is a very important habit that most people in our society have not developed. Lack of exercise is a major problem and a contributing factor in many of the preventable diseases that many Americans have.

The right amount of exercise helps to prolong life, reduces stress, and increases the release of endorphins which ultimately contribute to our happiness.
Exercise is one of the best ways to blow off steam. When someone doesn't have activities to do to blow off steam, they usually end up arguing with others; especially those that they are intimately involved with.

I found the following statement on livestrong.com: "The recommended amount of exercise is only 30 minutes of moderate exercise or 15 minutes of vigorous exercise per day. However, only 32.5 percent of American adults are meeting these

guidelines, says the Center for Disease Control."

Therefore, nearly 70% of the US is more than likely unhealthy. An unhealthy body usually has an unhealthy mind, which leads to unhealthy habits.

Read more at: http://www.livestrong.com/article/262489-the-leading-causes-of-obesity-in-america/#ixzz2CiIDbAJq

#3 – You regularly eat unhealthy foods. Most people know that it is not good to eat unhealthy foods on a regular basis. Other than the lack of exercise, this may be the leading cause of obesity. Poor food choices are a habit that has become the new normal in our society; partly due to the advertising and marketing of fast food chains.

You are what you eat.

You are what you eat physically, mentally, spiritually, financially, and emotionally. Therefore, taking in undesirable and unhealthy foods of any kind, can only lead to unhealthy and undesirable output.

At times in my life when I have strayed away from a healthy diet, it has negatively affected my attitude, mood, and energy. Someone that eats unhealthy on a regular basis is more prone to DIS-EASE and therefore on a cellular level, they are unhealthy in their attitude, thoughts, mood, and overall energy levels.

Dealing with a person like this on a regular basis is not easy. Therefore, if a person doesn't want to marry you, it may be because they don't want to take part in your unhealthy eating habits or risk the possibility of being influenced by them.

#4 – You have a family disease (heredity) that I can't deal with. One time in a relationship I had to make the decision on whether or not a person that had a disease that neither they or I had any control of, would cause me to make the decision to move forward with them or not. While the disease would not affect my person, having children could potentially put the child at risk of multiple difficulties concerning their health.

Well, needless to say, I made the choice to continue with the relationship and a little over a year later, a child was born. While he may carry the potential for disease, he is healthy and has no real threat of serious health conditions from the decision that was made by his father and mother to stay in the relationship and produce him.

However, in many cases, an individual may make the opposite decision. If you are more fearful of the possibility of a negative outcome than you are a positive one, it may not be a good thing to stay in the relationship.

If the person you are dating doesn't want to marry you, a family disease may be the reason they don't want to marry you.

#5 – Don't take care of your teeth. The teeth are very important to your overall health and well being. As a young child you don't understand this. Then, as you

get into your late teens and twenties and have to have a tooth or two removed, you realize the importance of every single tooth in your mouth. The body is connected. Every part is important. Your teeth are connected to nerves that are connected to different parts of your body. Therefore, the health of your teeth is important to the overall health of your mind and body.

My mother is what I call a "teeth person." She almost always will not entertain a man that doesn't take care of his teeth. Even if your teeth aren't straight, brushing and flossing them on a daily basis is important. Take care of what you have. Why? *When you take care of what you have, what you have will take care of you.*

Having tooth pain is probably the most excruciating pain there is. The biggest and strongest man can be brought to his knees from tooth pain. Tooth pain almost impairs your ability to do anything. Your only desire becomes getting rid of the pain.

Also, when you kiss someone, you usually want their breath to smell decent. When it is not, you usually have some issues with your teeth. Oral hygiene is important. All people that I know at some point even if it is only in the morning have bad breath. However, this can become a serious issue if your teeth aren't properly cleaned on a daily basis.

If the person you're dating doesn't want to marry you, it may be because you don't take care of your teeth. I know my mother wouldn't marry you!

#6 – You don't take regular baths and keep your Body Hygiene in order. One of the questions in 99 Questions was, *"How often do you bathe?"*

I usually got a whole lot of laughs from this question because it was usually the first question people would see when they opened the book.

There are men and women that are attractive, but are not married because they don't take regular baths. If they do, they may have a body odor or scent that is not pleasing to others that people just can't get past. People can deal with bad breath sometimes, but dealing with body odor is a whole different issue.

It is offensive to walk around knowing that you have not taken a bath for multiple days. Your own scent should begin to become offensive to you. If you are able to take a bath, take one. If not, the person you're dating will probably begin to become less attracted to you. And...this easily fixable problem may be the reason that they WILL NOT MARRY YOU!

Mental Reasons

"A mind is a terrible thing to waste!" This is the slogan for the United Negro College Fund and a very true quote indeed. However, many of us waste and misuse one of the most powerful things we have, our mind.

"The body manifests what the mind harbors."
~Ancient Proverb~

#1 – Your IQ. Your Intelligence-Quotient or IQ is a number or score derived from one of several standardized tests designed to assess intelligence.

Most egg/sperm donor facilities require your IQ and educational history along with your health history in the application and acceptance process. It is believed that a father's and a mother's IQ can be hereditarily passed on. Therefore, even in relationships, there are those that will not date a man or woman that they feel is too intelligent or not intelligent enough.

This can pose an issue in a relationship. Two of the young ladies that I spoke of earlier in the book, would often feel that I was much smarter than they were.

One in particular, would cause issues at times because she felt that I would be a little condescending when I would talk to her. I didn't understand because I was just being me. I felt that she was intelligent and a very smart person. So, out of respect, when I spoke to her I would always approach her in that manner. This would make her a little uncomfortable when it came to situations or fields that she had no knowledge of. As opposed to letting me know that she didn't, she would just get upset with me and let me know I was being condescending or act as if she did know and then go look up things later on her own. She would then come back and question me and challenge me on the subject since she all of the sudden had read something on the internet.

Looking back, this was the source of many of our arguments. When, in reality, it should always be a good thing to have someone that is well versed in things that you aren't. You should applaud people for what they know, and encourage them to learn more in areas that they don't know much about.

I don't know what Henry Ford's IQ was, but I think he was smart. He was able to pull together people smarter than he was to help him accomplish what he was trying to do. He became extremely successful by doing so. His wife was the catalyst. She could have easily discouraged him, but instead she encouraged

him. Her IQ may have even been higher than his. Whether her IQ was higher than his or not, she was able to live very well because of the efforts of his mind.

#2 – A mental issue such as bipolar or schizophrenia. This is a serious decision to make when you have been dating someone and find out they have a mental disorder. Sometimes, something such as bipolar disorder can go unnoticed and untreated. Therefore, even the individual that has it may not even know.

If you are dating an individual that seems to have multiple personalities, understand that he/she may have not been treated yet, or they may have been and haven't divulged that information to you.

Certain situations in life can be so mentally traumatic that it can cause an individual to have a nervous breakdown. These situations can cause mental issues such as depression that must be treated or will cause a continuous downward spiral of the person's mental health.

A person that is mentally unstable can be a risk factor to both the other person and themselves. If you suffer from a mild to serious mental disorder, this may be the person you're dating won't marry you.

#3 – Lack of Intellectual stimulation. Many women state that intellectually stimulating conversation is one of the important desires they seek in a mate. More and more men that want to get married also seem to feel the same way. Why? Without it, many feel that there can be no long lasting connection. For the intellectual, this is usually very important. It is important that they are able to exchange ideas and philosophies. It is important that they can have the person that they will more than likely spend the majority of their time with, be able to have a conversation that is intellectually stimulating.

#4 – We think too differently about life & certain situations. Sometimes intellectually stimulating conversation can be great between two individuals, but there can still be constant disagreement about how each one looks at the same situation.

When this happens, couples that have very strong personalities can become very bullish towards one another. This can cause the breakdown of communication between them and they can begin to become adversaries.

I was out one day promoting at a somewhat upscale supper club in Addison, TX, and a small group of young ladies and men were having a conversation. The conversation ended. Then, about 10 minutes later, a couple of the young ladies came back through and one of them said, "See what the problem is, you men cannot handle a strong woman." I laughed and said, "That's not true. We love a strong woman. What we can't handle is a disrespectful woman."

Sometimes, because everything has the potential to become personal, a woman can go into combat mode when a man actually has an intellectual opinion or an

opinion of his own that is opposite of hers.

When this happens, disrespectful and argumentative tones and attitudes can follow as if she is having a conversation with one of her girlfriends. Many times, a woman has to realize that a man is not your girlfriend. Certain things can't be said and certain tones can't be used in normal conversations. If they are, you begin to become less and less attractive to a man the more this happens.

Since there has been this EQUAL WHEN IT'S BENEFICIAL type of attitude that some women have taken, attitudes and behaviors like this have been a detrimental factor to the long-term success of the relationship. Both people in the relationship can't always have an EGO. It must be a middle ground and mutual respect when it comes to conversation. If not, the man/woman will eventually begin to share less and less of his/her intellectual thoughts, ideas, and feelings with you.

13

Financial Reasons

#1 – You don't have a source of income (Job, business, etc.). Not having money in a society where so much emphasis is put on having it can cause a serious issue in relationships for both men and women.

Because their seems to be more and more of a gap being created between the "Have's" and the "Have Not's," when a man or a woman doesn't have a source of income it can be a bit of a turn off. Many women, in today's time, still feel that a man is supposed to take care of them financially. Men don't mind taking care of a woman, but it is surely appreciated when a woman is able to take the "WE" mentality versus the "ME" mentality. Meaning, I am here and I appreciate you wanting to take care of me, but at this time in our life we have a plan that will work out much better if I am able to financially contribute; even if it is only a little bit.

One of my childhood friends is a very smart and intelligent woman. She is now a lawyer. Her husband is very able to take care of her and does, but she goes to work every single day. She still contributes to the household as if she absolutely had to. She doesn't take on the mentality that some women in her same financial position or less would do; YOUR MONEY IS OUR MONEY and MY MONEY IS MY MONEY!

On the other hand, there are multiple women that are making more money than men or just as much now-a-days. With nearly 50% of the U.S. workforce being comprised of women, it is easy to see how this could be a problem for many men and women in their relationships.

Multiple women that make yearly incomes above $100,000 have stated that the man they want to be with has to make that same kind of money or more. They have stated that the man has to have what they have. He must have a house, the same salary or greater, the same level of vehicle, the same level of education or higher, or they don't want to date him and definitely not marry him. The question by most men has always been, "If you have all of this, what do you need me for?" Or..."If you have this already, why do I have to come into the relationship with it already?"

A woman wants to FEEL SECURE. When thousands of women I've interviewed or conversed with

were asked to define secure, ***money*** was in the answer. FINANCIAL SECURITY is extremely important for a woman's mind to feel secure. Unless a financially secure woman is a woman that is secure within her own self, much like first lady Michelle Obama, it could be very difficult for her to marry a man that is not financially secure.

The First Lady said in an interview that Barack didn't promise her money, riches, homes, etc., but he did promise her an interesting life. And she said that he fulfilled his promise. He picked her up in car that was drivable, but was a jalopy. Had she judged him by the car he was driving, he or she may not be where they are right now.

However, the woman that you're dating will probably say "You're nothing like Barack Obama." And the man you're with will probably say, "You're no Michelle Obama..." If you don't have a source of income or a high paying job, this may very well be the reason why the person you are dating doesn't want to marry you.

#2 – Poor money management skills or I don't like the way you manage money. Sometimes, actually most of the time, people manage their money differently. Everyone has different money management habits. This has a lot to do with what we were taught in our homes growing up or what we decided to do once we left our parents house.

In marriages and most cohabitating relationships, this tends to be a constant source of arguments or disagreements. There is not a central source of education on money management in high schools or colleges in our society. Money has certain rules, but most of us don't come from households where money was managed well. If it was, our parents rarely spoke of it.

Sometimes, two individuals can both manage money in a way that works for them individually, but in a relationship the way that both people manage money together is more important than how they manage it separately.

People divorce for this reason and/or seek counseling concerning money rather often. Managing money as a couple needs to be taught because when it is done well, the couples are able to get ahead financially much faster than they can separately. However, when they don't, they seem to move ahead financially very slowly or not at all.

If you don't manage your money well, this may be the reason the person you're dating won't marry you.

#3 – Poor Credit. This is a serious issue for a man or woman that is dating an individual that doesn't have good credit. It is very easy to mess your credit up now-a -days. If you get sick, take a trip, or just so swamped with life and miss a payment or two on a couple of items, your credit score will be negatively affected.

Now, if you lose your job, get your car repossessed, evicted, or your home gets foreclosed on, your credit will be even more negatively affected. This

is a cycle that can be very difficult to recover from and some people have even committed suicide during hard times like this.

One thing I always tell people is this, "CREDIT CAN BE IMPROVED." Certain things about a person can't be improved. Because it can be improved, don't make a permanent decision over a temporary situation. Bad credit is a temporary situation as long as you have a plan to improve it. If you have a plan, I have realized that it will improve much faster than you think.

There are many credit improvement plans out there. Research the ones that are best for you. You can also, call and make payment plans with your creditors; they will usually work with you. Many of them will even take settlements on accounts. Depending on the age of the account and the creditor, some of the settlement amounts can be as low as 10 cents on the dollar. Whatever you choose to do, educate yourself, make a plan and stick to the plan. Your credit will improve.

If the person you're dating won't marry you, it may be because your credit is not good.

#4 – You have money problems too often. Have you ever known someone that was always having money problems? If you're like me, the answer is "YES!" If you're really like me, at some point in your life, that person was the person you look at in the mirror every single day.

An associate that I mentioned in one of my other books had two jobs, a nice car, and a good apartment.

He seemed to be doing well financially by outside appearances. However, he often had money problems. He had just as many money problems as someone that made less money than he did. The good news is, after a couple of years, he got a break. He was promoted to a position that paid him enough to do a little more than just make ends meet.

There are times in life that no matter how good our financial habits may be, or how disciplined we are with sticking to our budgets; we consistently seem to have issues surrounding money. These periods of time can sometimes be short periods, and at other times, they can seem to last for years. When it is the latter, you definitely can feel like you are treading water. You may feel like every step you take forward, you take two steps backwards.

Trying to keep a positive state of mind during these periods can be hard, but it is the most important way to go through these times. Just know that if the person you're dating doesn't want to marry you, it may be because you have money problems too often.

#5 – Don't pay your bills on time. This is one of those money habits that seem basic. However, depending on where you are financially in your life and what you have been disciplined to do, both will determine whether or not you pay your bills on time.

Sometimes it is not possible for people to pay their bills on time for different reasons. One of those could be that they don't have enough money to actually pay their bills; called "Robbing Peter to pay Paul."

For a person that likes to make sure they pay their bills on time, being with a person that doesn't feel the same way can be quite stressful. No one wants to have undue stress like the lights being turned off because the bill wasn't paid and the money was actually available.

Simply put, if the person you're dating doesn't want to marry you, it may be because you don't pay your bills on time.

Learning how to lower your bills and increase your income is well worth the time that it takes to develop this habit and skill.

#6 – Don't have a checking or savings account. In his movie, *Laugh at My Pain*, Comedian Kevin Hart, let the world know that he has a checking and a savings account. The movie is quite funny if you have seen it.

To some people, not having a checking or a savings account is still a practice that is safer to them than having one. In the south, many people used to keep their money in their house. It was usually kept under the mattress, a combination or key safe, under the floorboard, or another secret place that no one knew about.

In our modern times, not having a checking or savings account makes it hard to be able to do business. It is almost impossible and time consuming to do business without a bank account because most businesses require a debit or credit card. The invention of the prepaid debit/credit cards have allowed people to do business without an actual bank account. Conversely, the cost of doing business this way is more expensive than most people realize.

Having a bank account is a smart decision. If you don't have a checking or savings account, this may be the reason the person you're dating won't marry you; especially if you can't get qualified for one or don't desire to have one.

#7 – You don't have insurance (Health & Life, Home & Auto). Living life without insurance is not a smart decision for anyone. For example, auto insurance is a necessity in most states and a good investment. For a small amount of money per month, you are able to protect yourself and others against unknowns. Driving a car without insurance can actually be very detrimental. I was once arrested because I absolutely didn't have enough money to buy any insurance for my car, and the law had just been put into effect that all vehicles on the road had to have insurance.

I had just gotten a job, was trying to keep my car, my apartment, and my life together at that time in my life. This was before I wrote 99 Questions. I had just turned 26 and was struggling to hold on to the life that I had become accustomed to.

Hurricane Ike

In 2008, one of my nephews was having a birthday party at my mom's house. Hurricane Ike was heading north and ended up hitting my hometown of Texarkana, TX. I was coming home for my 10 year

reunion. I left the reunion and headed straight back to Dallas in the storm at the leading of my inner voice; as opposed to going back to my mom's for the birthday party.

While they were having the party, the Hurricane caused one of three 200+ year old oak trees in her yard to be uprooted and fall on the house. Needless to say, the house was severely damaged on one side of the house. Like many good decisions she made on her teachers salary over the years, my mother had good home owner's insurance. The house was able to be fixed. Had she not been paying insurance for the last 20 years or so, the house would have been a loss and she wouldn't have been able to pay for the repairs out of her pocket.

Life, health, and dental insurances are also important. Paying for insurance can seem like a waste of money until you actually need it. Then it seems like the best investment that you could have made. Insurance of all kinds' help you hedge against loss. Therefore, it ultimately saves you so much more money than it actually costs you.

Having these things as a man helps the woman to feel more secure; even if you're not making an abundant amount of money. Having good benefits will definitely help you and your potential mate to feel a little better about your responsible financial choices.

If you don't believe in having insurance, this may be the reason the person you're dating will not marry you.

#8 – Bad spending habits (clothes, shoes, gadgets, etc). This is an issue that men and women of all ages may have. We learn most of our habits concerning money from our parents. Even the words that we use when it comes to money usually originate from our parents. However, sometimes, when we get out of our parents house and begin to make our own money, we do things differently. This is not always the best thing. We try and keep the same habits that we had when we lived with our parents, and realize that our disposable income is not the same as it used to be.

We still try to use our money to buy new clothes, shoes, phones, eat out, go to the movies, etc., but don't think about how much it really costs to live on our own. Many times, we still have to borrow money from our parents into our late 20's.

Here is why:

- First REAL Job = $40,000/year before taxes
- Real Pay = $32,000/year after taxes
- Rent = **$750/month**
- Lights, Water, Gas, Trash, Cable, Internet, Phone = **$500/month**
- Car note & Insurance = $350 + $150 = **$500/month**
- Food = $100/week = **$400/month**
- Hair care products & cuts, deodorant, soap, tissue, cleaning supplies, etc. = **$100/month**
- Gas for vehicle = $60/week = **$240/month**
- Student loan payments = TOO MUCH???

We graduate. Get our first job. Get our apartment. Get a car. Get new furniture. Get new

clothes for our new job. This causes us to be financially in the red before starting our first job. But, since most of us have been so used to having our parents support us, we continue our old habits. The rest of us realize that we have to develop a plan very quickly in order to get caught up; starting first and foremost with our spending habits.

Now, there are multiple people that have bad spending habits that don't live above their means. Because they have developed the habit of using nearly all of their resources on things they don't need, they don't recognize the need for savings until it is too late.

If you have bad spending habits, this may the reason the person you're dating won't marry you.

#9 – You live above your means. One of my friends is very frugal. She doesn't believe in living above her means at all. I totally understand her. Sometimes, I even believe that she takes it a little too far. However, what I do know is that she does a great job at taking care of herself and her little girl.

In less than a 2 year period, she moved to Dallas, TX, got a job, bought a house, got a new car. Her credit is very good and she will budget down to a quarter. She carpools and everything. She kept the same car for over 10 years. The car had rust on it. She is 31. She would not claim to be the smartest person in the world, but she follows very basic principles and rules concerning money. All of which I think yield her a great return in the area of being able to live comfortably.

The other side to living above your means is to create a way to increase your means. My great-grandfather would say, ***"There are two ways to get ahead in life. Make more than you spend or spend less than you make."***

If you live above your means, this may be the reason that the person you're dating will not marry you.

#10 – Cash flow issue. As I learned in my finance course with Dr. Jules King, CASH FLOW IS THE NAME OF THE GAME. The wealthy are taught this. He taught us that CASH FLOW solves problems.

I later read the same principles in the bestselling book, Rich Dad, Poor Dad, by Robert Kiyosaki. Dr. King was the professor on campus that made more money than all of the professors in the business department. The saying, "Those who can't do teach..." definitely didn't apply to him. He never ran a business. He invested in real estate and learned to invest in stocks, bonds, mutual funds, hedge funds, options, etc. He learned to evaluate a piece of property and a company extremely well. He taught us that it came down to the cash flow. If a company was having financial problems it usually boiled down to the cash flow.

In my own life and in the life of my friends and family, when there are money problems, these issues can usually be solved by an increase in cash flow. This is why I have always thought it to be robbery for most teachers to get paid once a month. This is a cash flow problem. This is why teachers usually complain about the pay that they receive. The problem is really

not the pay in many cases, more than it is the regularity of the pay (cash flow).

Many small business owners and individuals that work in real estate or commissioned sales positions run into a cash flow problem. They don't have enough money to make it through the periods where they may not close a deal. Even in positions where there is a draw against commission, by the time the deals close, you may still end up owing the company money.

A long time friend of mine decided to become a commission only recruiter for a company about 5 years ago. She enjoyed the position, but found out the hard way just how important cash flow really was. She looked at the upside of the job, which I always advise, but she didn't look at what actually mattered...CASH FLOW. Unless you have another job or another source of income, this can be a hard road to travel. Not being able to get paid causes your mind to not be able to attract what you actually need, which starts a cycle; the cycle of having money, but no cash flow. Not knowing when a paycheck is going to come is not for the faint at heart, and not for the spouse of everyone.

During the 3 years or so that she worked this position; she went through a whole lot of learning experiences with her marriage. She has been married now for over 30 years. She joked with me one time about life and how even after being married for so long, you are still learning yourself and your partner. She often says, "Armani, MARRIAGE IS WORK! But well worth it!"

If you have a cash flow problem, this may be the reason that the person you're dating won't marry you.

One Way to Establish Wealth

Quick Story: One of the individuals that I met when I was about 20 years old living in Rolla, MO, was a millionaire. I ended up becoming friends with him and his family. He was a really good guy. I found out that he and his wife had worked together to become wealthy. She worked in accounting. He worked in commission only door-to-door sales. He said that they saved up $70,000 in one year. I asked how they did it. He told me, "We had a plan. We lived off of her salary of about $40,000 and every time I was able to get a check, we banked it."

As simple as this plan is, you'd be amazed to find that there are so many people that are not willing to do this. The plan worked. She didn't have to work to much more after that, and was able to stay home and be a housewife. He then had the money to open up a business, improve credit, and make some investments.

They had done this many years prior to my meeting them. However, the same principle can work today. He had a cash flow problem. She didn't. They were able to be disciplined enough to make their plan happen. I believe that it also helped that she worked in accounting and understood money. She also understood sticking to a simple plan and how important cash flow and cash on hand really is.

#11 – You lie about your use of money. One of my Facebook friends posted a story about two engaged individuals. She had a friend of hers email her asking what she should do about a situation.

The man and woman had been saving up money for a down payment for a house and a small wedding. They had been saving up the money for almost 2 years. They had gotten up to $60,000. In a matter of a few months, she had used *a little here and a little there* as she put it, and the account balance was now around $14,000.

They had done all of the right things. They had a plan, agreed to the plan, worked towards the plan, made automatic deposits into the account straight from their paychecks, and now because of her inability to delay gratification and actually lie without telling him, used over $40,000 on different things that don't have any real value.

I don't know the outcome of what happened at the time of this writing, but I would definitely believe that he wouldn't be marrying this woman.

My response to this woman was to first and foremost sell everything that she had bought. Then, get a second job and the entire check would have to go towards that account. Third, live off of half of her income and increase the amount of direct deposit into the joint account. Fourth, go seek counseling. Fifth, tell her fiancé what she did.

What would you do?

#12 – **You've made money your God and/or your identity.** If you make money your god, you'll never be satisfied with money because you'll never have enough.

There is nothing wrong with desiring money. However, when you are worshipping money, you'll do almost anything to have. You will lose all of your morals for the attainment of it. Only to see that it is fleeting.

When a person's identity is linked only to money if they were to ever not have it, it is very possible that they could go into a deep depression and even become suicidal. As international music artist and actor Drake said, "Just enough to solve your problems, too much will kill you."

If there is nothing interesting about you other than money, male or female, it may be the reason the person you're dating won't marry you.

#13 – No plans or desire to own things of value/ NO INVESTMENTS. Whether you have a lot of money or not, in our society, it seems like many of us tend to buy things that depreciate in value more often than we do things that appreciate. We seem to buy things that don't have any real value. We have a tendency to gravitate towards the purchasing of shiny things.

In most companies, cash on hand is listed as a liability as opposed to an asset. When I was first taking Accounting 101, I did not understand this. I didn't understand debits & credit nor assets & liabilities.

I knew that in order to be really wealthy, I would have to learn the language of money. I knew that I didn't have the language of money, finance, investments, or banking. I would have to at least learn to understand the financial statements; at some point. So, while I was in my first semester of college, I changed my major from Music to Finance.

By the time I was in my second year of college, I wanted to start investing and I did. I bought some of my own stocks for the first time. However, I lost my money.

Why? I tried to take a very small amount of information that I had just learned from my professor, Dr. Jules King, and didn't understand that there were different levels of investing and certain timings on different stocks. I learned the hard way. I got a learning experience. As I have learned, in life, you usually PAY for learning experiences. It is better to pay for education upfront than to pay later. It is kind of like insurance.

Had I waited until I actually was enrolled in my investment class, I would actually have made money because I would have learned the knowledge needed to make an educated and less risky decision. I would have been able to hedge against loss. The investment class would have been my insurance.

I was having a conversation with a lady I was dating about investing $1,000 in silver. I knew that at the time I was going to invest in silver that it was a good investment and at the time of this writing it still is. I was talking to her and she of course, shot the investment down. Her degree was not in finance, math or even business.

Therefore, the conversation probably would have been best to have never been started in the first place. I was sharing something that I thought would be good to talk about and hopefully help inspire her to want to invest with me as well. Conversely, she was adamant about it not being a smart investment and was so convincing that I didn't even invest. Sometimes, you want to keep your great ideas to yourself; especially when you're dating someone that doesn't have the same information that you do. Their limited knowledge on a subject and your desire to keep peace can sometimes not be a good mix.

If you are investing in something that will hold value that can be sold later for at least the amount that you paid for it, the risk is pretty low. Speak to a professional concerning your investments, not someone that isn't experienced in investing.

If you don't have investments or desire to have them in order to SECURE an income for a future time, this may be the reason the person you're dating won't marry you.

EDUCATIONAL REASONS

#1 – Don't like to read. Reading is fundamental. It is one of the best ways to expand your mental capacity and education. They say "***A reader is able to live a thousand lives, but if you're not a reader, you only live one.***"

Certain things happen to your mind as you read. Your mind is taken to a place that allows you to drift away into another reality or able to cope, and/or being inspired by the words of another.

Reading is also a form of insurance. When you read a manual for a product like a brand new car, you are taking precautionary measures to make sure that you know how to operate the vehicle. It is the same way with many products. However, most of the time, people want to learn the hard way. This usually causes issues that would not happen if the user manual was read prior to use or construction of the product.

The word *education* comes from the word *educe.* Educe means to extract, bring forth, or obtain. Therefore, in order for one to be educated, they must read to be able to have something to bring forth or extract something that is there.

If the person you're dating doesn't want to marry you, it may be because you don't like to read.

#2 – You have not completed your diploma or degree (bachelor, masters, doctoral). Certain people totally feel that they should not marry someone that has not completed the same level of formal education as they have. Others also feel that if the person didn't go to a particular college, then they are not worthy to be their spouse. Depending on the person and their long term goals, this could be a deciding factor on whether or not a person chooses to marry the person they're dating.

No plans to continue to improve your education (lifetime learner). The same childhood friend of mine that I spoke of earlier, also graduated top of her class and went to a prestigious college for pre-med and did a year in medical school prior to finally deciding to go to law school. If there was no such thing as formal education, both of us would still be lifetime learners. We love to know. We love to find out 'what is.' When we've talked over the years from the age of preteens to now grown parents, we have rarely had short conversations because we have each learned so much in

between the times that we didn't talk to one another. Our ideas change and grow. Our outlook on life and the knowledge and information that we gain improves. Therefore, our conversations can become quite interesting, fun, and sometimes controversial.

It has definitely allowed each of us for many years to be able to stand our ground with just about anyone. Whether you plan to continue your formal education or not, becoming a lifetime learner is extremely important. In this ever-changing world it can be difficult to stay up-to-date on even some of the basic changes and developments.

Therefore, if you have taken on the attitude that you have learned all that you need to learn in life, this may be the reason the person you're dating won't marry you.

#3 – Watch too much TV, idle time. I am going to assume that most of the women reading this book believe in a Supreme Being or source from which we all originate. Also, most have probably read Proverbs 31 and would consider themselves to be a Virtuous Woman. However, many don't understand exactly what that is according to the definition in the chapter.

Let's take a look at verse 27. *She looketh well to the ways of her household, and* ***eateth not the bread of idleness.*** Growing up I was taught, "And idle mind is the devil's workshop." I understand because when suggested by the wrong suggestion(s) and idle mind can become a very active body towards the wrong things. And idle mind is easily influenced.

One of the synonyms of **idle** is **inactive**. The more inactive one is, usually the more inactive one becomes. As I spoke of earlier in the book, inactivity or lack of movement and exercise has caused our society to become more and more obese; our minds included.

Many of us often complain about the lack of time to exercise, or the time we have to cook healthier meals. Zig Ziglar, who at one time was over 40 and overweight said, **"It is not the lack of time, it's the lack of direction."** Meaning, it is about what we chose to do with our time as opposed to how much time we think we have. Everyone has the same amount of hours each day.

According to Neilsen (the company that does the ratings for media) the average American watches more than 4 hours of TV per day. Meaning that out of a 168 hour week, more than 28 of them are used watching television. Meaning, someone else is TELLING you YOUR VISION. This time could easily be used to START REALIZING YOUR OWN VISION.

I have a program where I teach people how to write the first draft of their book in as little as 10 days. The only way they are able to do this is to be able to actually *follow the plan*. The plan that we create causes them to direct their time.

With the 28 hours per week or less that the average person uses to watch television, they could actually educate themselves or someone else. They could complete their degree or gain a new skill or certification of some kind.

If you watch too much TV or have absolutely too much idle time, this may be the reason that the person you're dating won't marry you.

#4 – You are Closed Minded/Not Well Rounded. A person that is closed minded and not willing to see life from another point of view is usually a person that has stopped growing educationally. Knowledge is infinite. Therefore, our understanding and experiences are also infinite. The amount of what we can actually learn is infinite. For years, scientists have said that we use a very small percentage of our brain. I don't know how true this is for everyone, however, in my own brain I know that there is so much more that I could learn.

Some people are not well rounded because they have never been exposed to anything outside of their current surroundings. ***The person that determines the diameter of your education determines the circumference of your world.*** This is how people are able to stay enslaved for centuries even without being physically enslaved. It always seems to be a surprise to the world when someone that doesn't have a degree from a major university or no degree at all becomes a millionaire because there was no formal teaching for this individual to become wealthy; based upon the education they were given.

The self-made millionaire has usually had to become open-minded and well-rounded to what they have never been exposed to. They have had to educate and somehow expose themselves to possibilities that were not in their immediate surroundings. They had to chart their own course on a path that they had never traveled or ever watched anyone else travel. They had to become a trailblazer.

If you are dating someone with an open mind and you don't have an open mind, this may be the reason why they won't marry you.

#5 – Poor Choices of Music. You may be thinking, "What does music have to do with education?" Well, music is one of the most effective ways of teaching. This is why most children first learn to sing their alphabet and numbers. For many individuals, a melody accompanied with a beat, causes the mind to memorize the message much easier.

This is the reason many of the children from the Hip-Hop generation can remember a rap song faster than they can their homework or lesson from school. Even as grownups, a song often seeps into our memory bank faster than work projects or college coursework.

This being said, what a man or woman listens to musically, may tell you much about their thoughts. You may be able to see much of what they listen to and watch on television reflected in their personal views, actions and words.

If the person has a poor choice of low vibratory music, or a poor choice of music, take a look at their personal affairs, and you can almost always see a parallel.

Family Reasons

#1 – You don't want children. A good friend of mine that I met just after her first divorce got remarried to the same person that she divorced a few years prior to getting remarried. Well, she recently divorced him again because he didn't want any more children. She did. He was much older than her. So, for him, he was probably thinking, "I do not want to go through this again." However, she is about 30, young and vibrant, attractive, and would make a great mother, but she doesn't have any children.

She often told me that she remarried him because she really loved him. I can understand the power of love. Conversely, her desire for a child was much stronger than the desire to stay married to a man that she really loved. Now, while this may not have been the only reason a divorce happened, I believe that this was the ultimate deciding factor.

Another friend of mine has a child and she doesn't want another child. Therefore, the man that gets with her will have to not want children. She is a wonderful mother and I think that it would be great for her to have some more children, but she feels that the age her daughter is at this point is a good age. She often tells me that she doesn't want to go through the diaper changes and breast feeding phase again.

An associate of mine told me this when I asked her about wanting to have children; "I only have enough love for my man. I'm not interested in sharing that love with children." So, all three of these women have three different outlooks on children and having and/or wanting children.

If you are a man or woman reading this, please know what you want up front as far as this part of life and relationships are concerned. It will help you and the other person to be on one accord and save the both of you undue emotional pain.

If the person you're dating doesn't want to marry you it may be because you don't want children and they do or that you want children and they don't. Either way, it would be well worth it to find out.

#2 – Have too many children already. Years ago, a woman told me that she could not marry a man that had more than one child because that would be too much money leaving her household. I thought this was

funny, but she knew what she wanted and what she didn't. Some men are the same exact way. Having a child changes the dynamics of the dating and the dynamics of the relationship; especially if the child is not your own.

Another woman stated that she wouldn't marry a man with more than one baby mama because she was not about to become the next.

In most states, the parent paying child support is usually paying out about 20% of their income to support the child. This means, if an individual has $50,000/year income, $10,000/year or $833/month is going to the other parent to support the child. If a man or woman has multiple children, even more than this will come from their income.

For a man, having the time that he has with the mother of multiple children, he may not like this too much. This has the potential to become an issue for a man; especially if he has no children or none by you.

#3 – Can't have any children. A man or a woman could be the individual in the relationship that is not able to have a child. I was watching an episode of *Keeping Up With the Kardishians.* In this particular episode, Chloe found out why she had not been able to conceive a child. She and her husband, Lamar Odom, had been trying for a while and nothing had happened.

Luckily, she went to the doctor and found out that she was not ovulating. She can have children, however, sometimes, there are certain situations that can cause either the man or the woman to be the contributing factor; causing no child to be conceived.

While this was a special case, I loved the way her husband handled the situation. He was supportive. On the other hand, there are both men and women that handle a situation of not being able to have a child in a totally different manner.

A man or a woman that wants to conceive their own child with the person they are married to, will more than likely not want to marry a person that they can't have children with. If this is the case, this may be the reason that the person you're dating won't marry you.

#4 – You don't treat your children well. At one point in my life, dating a woman with a child or children was not an option for me. One day, I was having a conversation with my mom about this and she told me, "Well, Armani...If she has children it is not necessarily a bad thing because you will be able to tell a lot about her by the way she treats her children. The way she treats her children will be a good indicator of how she may treat you." That was good wisdom for me at that time in my life, and I took it and ran with it. The next three women I dated all had children. She was right. The only thing that she forgot to tell me was, "Pay attention to how she talks to and about the father of her children because that is a good indicator of how she may one day talk to you."

A man that has children usually is not the primary caregiver of the child. So, being able to see how

a man treats his children when he is with them just as it is with a woman, is a great indicator of how he will treat you or your children; especially if you were to become the mother of his child.

If the person you're dating doesn't want to marry you, it may be because you don't treat your children or their parent very well.

#5 – You don't have a healthy relationship with your mother. Although I don't watch television that often, whenever I visit other people, I usually watch it and seem to get something to write about.

I was watching an episode of the show LOVE AND HIP HOP, Stevie J and his baby's mother Mimi, were receiving counseling. During the session they realized that many of their issues stemmed from the lack of a good loving relationship with their mother. Both of them had struggled for years with having never established a loving relationship with their mother.

According to the psychologist, Stevie Js promiscuity had much to do with there being no relationship between him and his mother. As I stated earlier in the book, we first learn how to love from a mother. It's a lot easier to have loving relationships with other women, for both men and women, when they have had the love of a mother in their life.

Conversely, on the same show, we also witnessed the relationship between Lil' Scrappy and his mother become detrimental to the survival of the relationship he had with his daughter's mother. Sometimes a relationship with your mother can be so close that even when you become a grown man/woman the mother may not be able to let go and understand her new role in your life. Many mothers can remain domineering in the child's life for many years after the child has grown up and left home.

#6 – You don't have a healthy relationship with your father. If you don't have a healthy relationship with your father, you usually struggle with multiple insecurities and hang-ups late into adulthood.

Fatherlessness in America is linked to the source of many issues we face in our society. After typing in the words "Fatherless in America" there were pages and pages of information on just how big of an issue this is.

Research has shown that multiple behavior, speech, and cognitive issues begin to show up in the child that doesn't have an active father from 3 months to 12 months of age. These issues are evident in comparison to the children that did have an active father beginning as early as 3 months old.

It has probably become the most difficult dilemma that we can't figure out how to solve. Either way, we are now going on nearly 3 generations where millions of fathers are absent in the home; some by choice and others not by choice. It negatively affects the entire economy.

On the next page is a table of the single parent households by race in the US for 2011.

Non-Hispanic White	25%
Black or African American	67%
American Indian	53%
Asian and Pacific Islander	17%
Hispanic or Latino	42%
Total	35%

According to the US Census Bureau, in 2011, there were 11.7 million single parent families in the US, **85.2%** of which were headed by a female. *(U.S. Census Bureau – Table FG10. Family Groups: 2011)*

I was just having a conversation with someone that said it would be better to live somewhere else than to learn to get along with the child's father and live nearby. This would allow the father and the child to have multiple hours of interaction on a daily basis that the child needs and allow her the help that she needed financially and supportively.

Many women, because they have not had a good relationship with their father, find it difficult to have a good relationship with the opposite sex. When there is no father in the home, it rarely allows a female child to experience the love of her father on a daily basis.

During the teenage years, when going from a little girl to a young lady, she desperately needs the attention and affection of her father. Her body and mind are both going through so many different changes that the reassurance and attention from her father is essential. If not, she will more than likely have sex early and engage in many activities that are not productive.

Also, when there is no man in the household, especially during the teenage years, a young lady doesn't know how to let a man lead the household. She has only seen a woman lead the household. Therefore, she doesn't know how to accept his role and if he hasn't had a man in the household, neither does he.

#7 – Not yet divorced aka STILL MARRIED or Separated. I did a speaking engagement at a popular salon in Mesquite, TX. The setting was quite intimate and people were there dealing with real issues. This particular night I seemed to be really connected, on a spiritual level, with the issues that were going on with most of the people in the salon.

So, towards the end of the event, there was a young lady that had a pressing question. After listening to her for a minute, a gentleman sitting on the same row, but not right next to her, said, "Let me go ahead and interrupt. The person she is indirectly talking about is me. It seems like no matter what I do, no how much I go to work, or do what she wants, she still is not satisfied." At this point a few words were exchanged back and forth between them. I then asked the young lady to stop talking for a minute because I wanted the man to be able to speak. He had not said anything the whole event and I wanted him to get it all out. After

hearing everything that he had to say, I could only say to him, "Do you LOVE her? And do you want to marry her?" He of course said, "Yes!" She also said the same thing. I then asked, "Is there an ordained minister in the house?" There was. I got excited and said, "Okay, well how about the two of you come on up and get married right now!" They both just sat there and looked at me. So, I said, "Come on up! You both said that you were serious and wanted to be married." He then said, "I can't marry her because I am still married to someone else."

That was the shock of the hour for me, and for a few other people that were in the room. The man had been with her for 7 years or so, and for whatever reason had not gotten a divorce. He said that he had been faithful and present in the household, and had even been a father figure to her children. He was obviously separated from his wife, but had not divorced her. Therefore, the one thing that this young lady really wanted, she couldn't have. She had the man, but could not be the man's wife because he was still joined to his wife by law.

Now, many women seem to date married men. Not like the situation that we see here, but married men that still have daily interaction with their wife and family. Men that pay bills, celebrate anniversaries with their wife, birthdays with their children, and sleep every night in the same bed with the woman they took vows with. Some people see no problem at all with doing this. Men also date married women.

However, when it comes to marriage, if the person you're dating won't marry you, this is probably the most legitimate reason for why they won't marry YOU! They can't because they are married to someone else.

#8 – Unhealthy family and home life that you have not yet recovered from. I spoke a little about this earlier in the chapter. Some individuals have dealt with so much family pain and trauma from the past, that unless they get extensive counseling and psychotherapy, they may not be able to function in a relationship of love. Their deductive reasoning skills may not be so great and they may perceive even the smallest issue as a big threat. Over a period of time, when not treated, a serious unhealthy pattern of behavior may develop.

For instance, one young lady that I dated for a couple of years, would always feel as if I was trying to corner her whenever we would be trying to have a conversation about an issue. The smaller the room that we were in, the more threatened she felt. Well, I wanted to understand this. My body language never said, "I'm going to hurt you." I never stated with words that I was going to hurt her, nor was my tone loud when we would have discussions. When I finally approached her concerning why she did this, she told me that a guy she dated in college would hold her down and restrain her.

Our brain seems to work through association. Much of our home and family life influences the reactionary behaviors we display in our present daily interactions through the process of association.

Therefore, if you're dating someone that and they don't

want to marry you, it may be because of the unhealthy home and family life of your past that is negatively effecting your present.

#9 – You mother and father are not still together. Over the years I have met multiple men that say, "IF her parents are not together, I CAN NOT MARRY HER!" I didn't understand why? I do now.

At one point in my life, I had never seriously dated a young lady whose parents were not still married. When I finally did, I saw the difference in the adaptability to change and ability to follow through on keeping agreements versus not keeping agreements. In comparison, which is something that I don't really like to do but will for illustrative purposes, the young ladies that came from homes where the mother and father were still together, these young ladies understood the words, "Word is Bond." Parents teach the children to be dependable and how to follow through and make good on their promises with other people. A man proves this point in his daily walk. A mother can teach this, but a man rarely lets a child off the hook just because they all of the sudden had a change of heart or don't feel like doing something for someone.

Many people want to be able to depend on other people, but don't want to prove that they are also dependable. They want their mate to be committed to them, but don't want to commit. Our ability to stick to things and not quit, is a learned behavior from our parents/surroundings. Our idea of love and gender roles is first introduced to us by our parents. Even our conflict resolution skills are taught to us by our parents;

directly or indirectly. Having said this, I can now see why it's the choice of some people not to marry a person whose parents are not still married.

#10 – A History of Negative issues in the family. I spoke of this in another part of the book. Just as there are characteristics that we get from our parents and genetic disorders that we are predisposed to. there are also negative mindsets and other issues that we are predisposed to as well. For the most part we can't change our genealogical make up. You are the sum total of all the mother and fathers of your mother and father. So, if there is a history of eczema, hay fever, sickle cell, cancer, diabetes, heart disease, obesity, mental disorders, and many other genetically predisposed issues that could be passed down; The same goes for anything. Just know that this may be the reason that the person you're dating may not marry you.

#11 – You have very little to no communication with other immediate family members. Your family doesn't get along. Family is a very important piece to life and relationships.

If you are trying to get married to someone that has chosen NOT to have communication with their family members, this is a red flag. If it was for something extreme such as a killing of a family member, or attempted murder, or something very severe, I may be able to understand. However, when most people do this with their family, they will definitely do the same thing when it is not family. You are not family. You need to make sure that if this is you, figure out what the real issue is, and work on the

situation with your family because how can you start a family if you can't even communicate with the family you already have?

If you don't have a good relationship with your family, this may be the reason the person you're dating won't marry you.

#12 – You are a different race or cultural background. For some people this may pose a serious issue. I am a firm believer that love has no color. While more and more people today are of multiple races, there are those that still have not accepted the marrying of someone of a different race or culture. I like to see people interact with one another from all races, creeds, and cultural and socioeconomic backgrounds. We live in a world of contrast. The downside to this could very well be that whole cultures would be lost in the process of marrying into different cultures and races.

While that would take quite some time to happen, it could be possible. But for now, I say as I've always said, "Marry for LOVE." At the end of the day that is all that stands the test of time.

The fact that the two of you are from different races or cultural backgrounds may be the reason that the person you're dating won't marry you.

#13 – I Don't Get Along with Your Family. This is one issue that I see often between multiple families. It doesn't matter their race, age, religion, or economic status, dealing with family members can be an issue. Most of this happens because most of the times, when people talk to their family members about a problem in the relationship, the family members usually get involved. This causes more problems and adds fuel to the fire. The thing that I have noticed is the family forgets that these two individuals are family or working toward becoming a family. If a person is still involved with an individual obviously they love them or still want to be with them. As opposed to family members being the safe haven for one another every single time, they need to get the individuals into couple's counseling and motivate them to work through whatever issues they seem to be having.

I personally encourage couples to call their family members with good news and about the good times that individuals are having. This will easily help to alleviate some of the disdain. Sometimes, mothers or fathers don't want to see their children marry someone for whatever reason it may be. Then, they can cause problems within the relationship because of their disapproval of the person.

They want what they want for their child, and will many times push and push and even totally disassociate themselves from their children because of this. Usher Raymond openly did an interview with his mother on Oprah. His mom did not show up to his wedding because she was in total disagreement with the marriage of her son to his now ex-wife.

This particular reason is a reason that will go away or have to be totally ignored. Either way, if one or the both of you don't get along with each other's family members, this may be the reason the person you're dating won't marry you.

Relationship Reasons

#1 – You've cheated on every other person that you've dated. They say that the best way to predict the future is to look at the past. While this may not be the case all the time, the past is a good indicator of POSSIBLE future behavior. Why? We are creatures of habits. Unless something happens, usually traumatic, we usually think that what we are doing is ok. We believe the habits we have are just fine.

When it comes to this reason, I have seen multiple women and men complain that the reason they cheated was the fault of the other person. If you have not shown yourself to have been faithful in all of your previous relationships, how could you convince someone else that you would be faithful to them?

If the person you're dating won't marry you, it

may be because you have been unfaithful in your previous relationships.

#2 – Afraid of commitment. Okay...Let's see. Most men can be very afraid of commitment. Women of today seem to be afraid of commitment as well. In a society where everything is no contract, no commitment, no risk, try before you buy, or if you don't like it we'll refund your money, method of operation; it is very possible for both men and women to be AFRAID of COMMITMENT.

I often believe that men are afraid of commitment because of two reasons:

1. We want our FREEDOM
2. We don't want to be hurt AGAIN

Marriage is a serious commitment for a man that decides on his own to get married. He is usually marrying to be married to the woman that he has chosen. It seems to be more about the wedding, honeymoon, and the 'pomp and circumstance' for many women. But for a man, if we have actually taken the time to ask you to marry us, we are for real and are ready at the time we ask, to take that next step.

Men and women often expect more from the other person once they are married. There seems to be a sense of *"you should do this for me"* coming from both sides. When, in reality, it should be more of *"I'm going to do and be more of this for you"* coming from both individuals.

Marriages that seem to work are definitely more

about what they can give to the other person and less about what they can get from the other person. Both people are givers and committers that are committed to one another.

If one of you is afraid of commitment, this may the reason that the person you're dating won't marry you.

#3 – You've been unfaithful in the current relationship. The Bible asks in Proverbs, "Who can find a faithful man?" For a woman, this can be a difficult task. So, in a relationship, when there has been infidelity, it usually breaks the total trust of the relationship down. When there is no trust in the relationship, the individuals have to work really hard to rebuild it. Most of the time, when infidelity has happened in the relationship it is almost never forgotten by the man or woman.

If you have been unfaithful in the relationship with the person you're dating, this may be the reason that they won't marry you.

#4 – All of your relationships have ended on bad terms. This was something that I had to learn the hard way. This is actually one of those issues that can easily be looked over as a reason to *Never Date Someone*, let alone marry them.

If a woman or a man has had multiple relationships that have ended on bad terms, the common denominator is that particular person. Many times, they don't want to see it as their problem,

However, in many cases it usually is. The person is usually not able to see their contribution to the issues in the relationship and play the VICTIM.

If you can't take responsibility for your part in the relationship not being as good as it could have been, you are really wimpy. When you begin to blame all the issues that happened on the other person, you become like a child. The child always points the finger at the other person that hit them harder than they hit the other person. However, they rarely say, "Well I did hit them first."

This is even worse for those relationships that have ended badly where children are involved. If the mother or father treats one another badly and they have a child to take care of together, this is more than likely how your relationship will be if it ends and the two of you have a child together. Therefore, be mindful of this. Remember, "LIKE CAUSES PRODUCE LIKE RESULTS."

So, if the person you're dating doesn't want to marry you, it may be because each one of your relationships has ended on bad terms, or that you've blamed every relationship ending on the other person.

#5 – You don't have any friends or You don't have any long-term friends (unstable). – You burn your bridges. Each of these could be separate reasons why the person that you are dating won't marry you, but they kind of go together.

In order to have friends, you must show yourself

friendly. Even as a child, the children that don't have friends seem to not be that friendly. It doesn't mean that they aren't nice, they just are usually not perceived as being friendly. The same thing seems to happen to us as adults. The only thing that's different as an adult versus being a child is, you have had many years to learn how to be friendly and develop friendships.

You always want to know how long a man and definitely a woman's friends have been friends with them; especially their friends of the same sex. I always think that it is very important for a woman to have long time friends of the same sex. Friends that have been friends with them for so long that they are almost like sisters. This shows loyalty.

Having friends for long periods of time is a great sign of stability. Friendships that have stood the test of the time, allow you to grow. They teach you to be able to accept people for who they are and where they are in their life and still love and care for them. Longtime friends allow you to be able to see yourself transparently. They are usually able to check you and put you in your place like no other. They also help you learn how to communicate better with others.

People who tend to burn their bridges with others tend to be less transparent than those that don't burn bridges so often. When you are constantly burning bridges, you sometimes forget, that one day you have to go home and visit. You have to be able to have someone to vouch for you. Someone somewhere is going to have to be a character reference at some point in time.

When you can't get along with the same sex, to me it says a lot about you; Man or woman. I have stated to women on many occasions, **"Ya'll can't even get along with each other, but expect us (men) to get along with ya'll."**

I personally think that a man should always let the women in his family meet the woman he desires, and the women should let the men meet the man she desires. They will be able to see certain things that the opposite sex doesn't see.

If the person you're dating doesn't want to marry you, it may be because you don't have any friends, no long-term friends, or the fact that you burn your bridges.

#8 – I don't like the way you deal with the mother and/or father of your child/children.
Ok, I mentioned this a little bit earlier in this chapter. SO, it is pretty much self-explanatory. If you don't treat the mother or father of children well, how are you supposed to be able to treat someone else well?

Many women and men get this twisted. We get it twisted because we always point the finger. If you will be nice to someone that is trying to be nice to you as opposed to being mean, it will be very hard for there to be bad feelings towards one another. Most people think that a new relationship is going to solve all of their problems, and make the pain of the old one go away.

This is not true. The same issues will resurface in the new relationship. They will manifest in different yet

similar ways because you are the still the common denominator. And until you are able to take responsibility for this, you can do all the outside changes you want, you will still attract the same situations over and over again. Until you make a change on the inside and get rid of the bitterness, you will be of no real benefit to anyone for a relationship. You will keep experiencing the same things over and over again.

I will put this here for the purpose of impressing your subconscious mind, **"Like Causes Produce Like Results."** Therefore, if you see the person is not friendly and cordial with their child's father or mother, this may not be a good candidate for marriage or for you to have children with. If so, one day, this may very well be you.

If you treat the mother or father of your child/ children badly, this may be the reason that the person you are dating won't marry you.

#9 – None of your intimate relationships have lasted for long periods (i.e., 1-3 years). A man or a woman that has not been able to be committed for a year or more and they are in their late 20's or early 30's may not be a good candidate for marriage. This may not hold true for every situation, but it is better to think that it does hold true. It is kind of like 1,000 people saying "Hey, I got in the water and something bit me, but I didn't see anything in the water." At this point, people would rather test the waters and see for themselves. They would jump in and risk getting bit, to fill their curiosity.

If a woman is over the age of about 30 years of age, never been married and doesn't have children, I would say there is a reason. I would now say that if a man is over 40 years of age, never been married and doesn't have children, there is a reason.

Many times, people like this may be habitual liars, promiscuous, serial daters, and fault finders in others that are seeking perfection in imperfect people, or have serious mental and emotional issues that have gone untreated. There could be other reasons, but these are for the man and woman that say they want to be married and can't find anyone.

I just don't think that a woman gets past 35 and can't find someone or hasn't dated a really great guy that they could have married. And I don't think a man does that either.

If you have not had a long-term relationship prior to now, this may be the reason the person you're dating won't marry you.

17

10 Women All Men Should Run From

When I originally came up with the idea for this chapter, it was actually as a totally separate book. The subtitle for the book was, *"Which One Are You?"* The book was to be geared towards women that wanted to improve upon themselves and for men that were serious about finding a potential wife.

I often think that many books are not geared towards actually helping women and men create positive and effective change within themselves, but more or less geared towards selling books. Or about shifting the blame and playing games. It is easy to point the finger and blame the issues in the relationships entirely on men. I was always told by my mother, "It takes two to tango." What she was basically saying to me is, "both people are to blame for the problems within the relationship."

Instead of making this chapter a totally separate book, I decided that I would focus all of the energies on completing this book. Therefore, it became appropriate to just do a shortened condensed version of it in this particular chapter. In doing so, it allowed me to be able to create the chapter that will follow this one, ***5 Men You Should Never Marry***.

Each of these chapters is based upon ancient wisdoms and character traits that I have seen stand the test of the time.

Whether you are a reader or believer of the Bible or not, I believe that you will be able to benefit from both this chapter and the one to follow. I believe that you will be able to see yourself more clearly, even if but a little, and improve.

#1 – The Lying & Deceitful Woman

As stated in the earlier part of the book, a habitual liar is not a desirable trait for either a man or a woman. It was the most listed 'deal breaker' by both sexes. However, when a woman begins to tell lies, they seem to be the kind of lies that don't have to be told. They don't benefit her or anyone else. It is usually in the form of gossip and slander, and in many cases has the potential to put multiple people in danger.

While there may be some truth in the lie that is being told, there are usually more lies mixed with the truth that is being told than there is truth. The purpose and intention is to deceive the listener of these lies. Deceitful lies are told with the intent to turn people

against one another; especially mates, friends, and lovers. It is always good to ask a person telling you something negative about someone else, "WHAT IS THE PURPOSE OF YOU TELLING ME THIS?"

One of the things that was said about my great-grandmother at her funeral, by almost everyone that came up to speak, was that she wouldn't let you speak badly about someone that wasn't around to defend themselves. Her daughter, my grandmother, said she never heard her speak negatively about other people.

This was amazing to me because I remember her being a very sophisticated, yet humble, stern, confident, and a kind woman, that wouldn't even let her great-grandchildren say the words 'butt' or 'booty.' She wanted us to choose our words better. Knowing what I know now, she wanted us to use words that resonated on a much higher vibration when we expressed ourselves.

According to King Solomon, There are 6 things the Lord hates, 7 that are detestable:

- haughty eyes
- **a lying tongue**
- hands that shed innocent blood
- **a heart that devises wicked schemes**
- feet that are quick to rush into evil
- **a false witness who pours out lies**
- **a person who sows discord in a family**

Four of the statements above, deal with lying and deceit in some way. A man or woman that is continuously lying has the potential to steal, and a thief has the potential to murder or shed innocent blood. So, when you can cut the lie off early on, you will save a continuous spiral down effect.

"A false witness who pours out lies..." This is something that habitual liars and gossipers do; they pour out lies. When they do this, it usually sows discord in a family or between friends. In another translation it says, *"A false witness that speaketh lies, and he that soweth discord among brethren."*

People usually lie in order to get something or to keep from receiving punishment of some kind that they fear they may receive by telling the truth. Always allow people to tell you the truth and be willing to tell the truth. It makes things so much easier in the long run.

If the woman you're dating is a habitual liar and deceiver, you should run from her!

#2 – The Wayward Woman

The Book of Proverbs asks the question, "Why embrace the bosom of a wayward woman?" Let's look at the word wayward a little closer.

Here is one of the definitions that best fit what I believe King Solomon meant: *Difficult to control or predict because of unusual or perverse behavior.* Here are a few synonyms of the word **wayward** from www.merriam-webster.com:

- Rebellious
- ungovernable
- unruly
- disobedient

- willful (*or* wilful)
- incompliant
- Insubordinate

A man must be able to govern and control the affairs of his household if he is to be an effective leader and covering for his family. When there is a wayward woman in his household, he is not able to do this because she is ungovernable. She will not and refuses to stick to the plan. He is supposed to be able to first guide the woman and second govern. He can't do this if the woman is wayward.

A rebellious army is not and cannot be a successful army. A rebellious cast and crew for a director equal disaster. Where there is no vision the people perish. The vision usually comes through the man in the household. This vision usually includes the vision and long-term success of him, his wife, and their children.

A wayward woman and/or a contentious woman usually feels that she is equal to a man, and therefore doesn't have to adhere to any desires or rules that a man has concerning his household.

A man who is a happy man usually has a happy woman, and a woman that sees herself as a helpmate. She sees herself as a team player and just as important to the team. There is no need to have a quarterback if there is no one to throw the ball to. She understands that a man is not equal to her.

There are certain things that a man just can't do

as well as a woman. I don't care how hard he tries. And...the same applies to a woman. While we may have all been created equal, we are not all equal. Therefore, there are desires and rules that she has that he is also going to have to adhere to in order to make the household a serene and peaceful environment.

According to King Solomon, the wayward woman has a good use of seductive words. The word seductive comes from the word seduce, which means *to lead away from duty, accepted principles, or proper conduct.* The word seduction comes from Latin, which literally means ***"to lead astray."*** http://en.wikipedia.org/wiki/Seduction http://www.thefreedictionary.com/seduce

Other translations of the words *"wayward woman"* in Proverbs are:

- Promiscuous Woman
- Loose Woman
- Strange Woman
- Seductress

King Solomon says, "Surely her house leads down to death." A Wayward Woman is a woman that you should run from.

#3 – The Contentious & Angry Woman

The root word of the word CONTENTIOUS is the word, CONTEND. A few synonyms of the word contend are:

- Contest
- argue
- fight
- compete
- struggle

"*It is* better to dwell in the wilderness, than with a contentious and an angry woman."
Proverbs 21:19 ~KJV

When I first remember reading this in the bible, I was 26 years old. I had read it prior to this, but it didn't have any relevance to me. Having a father around or a man around to teach a man these things is always best.

However, King Solomon must have known of a time where there would be many men and women that would be raised without fathers.

A woman that has a father around and has been taught by the example of both her mother and father in the household knows when enough is enough. She understands that contending with her man doesn't produce unity or happiness in the household. It produces disunity, strife, and anger.

An argumentative woman and a woman that is angry is one of the worst things that a man could ever deal with. I don't know one man that enjoys this. It doesn't matter his race, creed, education level, financial wealth, religion, or culture, it is not a desirable trait. It eats away at the fabric of a man. It tosses him 'to and fro' to the point of never being able to rest his mind or spirit to produce and realize his vision.

A good friend of mine has high blood pressure because of his dealings with a contentious and angry woman. He is only 33 years old. His doctor told him that it was basically a matter of life or death situation for him to get his blood pressure down. He had to leave the relationship for his health.

If a man says, "Yes!" and she says, "No!" for the sake of being disagreeable, and for no real reason, she is a contentious woman. There are multiple women that do this. It's nothing new. If she purposely sets herself against you, your plans, and your goals, dreams, and aspirations, she is a contentious woman. If she complains about everything you do, no matter how good it is, or how hard you try to please her, she is a contentious woman. You will never be able to satisfy her. You will go crazy trying to do so. She is unhappy within herself, and will do all she can, knowingly or unknowingly to make you and any other man that she dates unhappy. You will be the man that she blames all of her problems on; even those problems that she has had in her life way before she ever met you. You will never be able to live down any mistakes that you have made; no matter how small they are. Again, you will have no rest. You will not be able to think clearly. RUN!

#4 – The Selfish & Entitled Woman

The woman that has the sense that someone owes her something just because she is a woman is the wrong kind of woman to marry. She is a lot like the woman that could not keep her feet at home. She spends her young years looking for a man to take care of her, with no desire to do the same in return.

She expects that just because she gives a man sex, whether she is married to him or not, but definitely if she is married to him, that he is supposed to

financially take care of her. Some are even made to believe this in the in their own churches, communities and religious organizations. I cannot find this in the Bible, Qur'an, Torah, or any other scripture of the major religions.

However, in the Bible, I can easily find the virtuous woman. The virtuous woman or wife, depending on the translation, was a woman that worked while she was young. She was what most of us today would call a 'hustler' or a woman that had the entrepreneurial spirit. She was a "helpmate." She understood her role as a helpmate in the household and outside the household. As one woman said, "She was a BADD WOMAN." She is the standard for many men desiring a wife, just as Boaz or Christ, may be for many women desiring a husband.

Often times, women that are seeking a Boaz type of man, forget that Ruth was a woman who had made good on her first commitment with the husband of her youth; she stayed with him until death parted them. She was also loving, obedient to wisdom, and committed to her mother-in-law. A quality you can't teach. Her heart was right. She was not lazy or looking for a handout. She was found working on the field of Boaz. I repeat, she was found working and not looking for a handout.

He had heard about her commitment to her mother-in-law and what had happened concerning her deceased husband upon his return to the city. He, out of respect and a willingness to honor his deceased family members, told her to stay on his field and work so she would be safe. He was able to see how she appreciated little. If you're faithful over little he will make you ruler over much. Because of her commitment, loyalty, work ethic, and appreciative spirit, she was able to BE FOUND by BOAZ.

The following is from the Book of Ruth: Then he said, *"Blessed are you of the LORD, my daughter! For you have shown more kindness at the end than at the beginning, in that you did not go after young men, whether poor or rich. And now, my daughter, do not fear. I will do for you all that you request, for all the people of my town know that you are a virtuous woman."*

A woman that has a sense of entitlement will never be satisfied, no matter how much you do for her. She will not let you rest because she will not rest. More, more, more is all she will scream and your days will be filled with nagging until her request is filled. Then more nagging until her newest request is fulfilled. This cycle will keep you in constant pursuit of something you cannot have with her; Peace & contentment of mind.

One female respondent wrote: ***"I am not sure I want to be married at this point because I am set in my ways and it's all about me and I treat myself a certain way. And the person I marry will have to treat me like I treat myself."*** 10/16/2012 1:52 AM

I am sure this individual is a very nice woman because most of the respondents are individuals that are familiar with my work and I with them. However,

this attitude of "ME, ME, ME" scares the right man away from you. Even if he can treat you the same way you treat yourself, none of what you said included the benefits of him treating you the certain way you treat yourself. There was no mention of reciprocity.

If you are dating a woman that is selfish and has a sense of entitlement, you should run before she runs from you and leaves you broke and disgusted.

#5 – The Woman that Thinks & Acts Like a Man
This is a woman that King Solomon doesn't mention. I am sure that there were a few women in his time that acted this way. However, she is very prevalent in today's society. She is the woman that ONLY NEEDS A MAN FOR SEX; and she may not need him for that.

She is what men would consider...
TOO INDEPENDENT.

This woman is and can be very cruel. There are men out there that like to try and break this woman down. She doesn't cry or show emotions in front of a man. She may not even show emotions that are considered weak in front of her female friends and family. In most cases, she has developed this behavior over the years. She says, "I love men, but I'm not letting anyone make me feel like I felt when..."

This "WHEN" experience may have been when she was young or older, but either way it is usually an event that took the emotions associated with showing love, out of her heart. She probably saw her mother or female friend or family member get beat or spoken to in a way that she felt she would never accept in her life. She may have been raised only by men. She may work in a male dominated workplace where she feels that she has to "cry outside."

A woman's strength is her femininity. It's in her being able to be a feminine woman, and being able to show her emotions that she feels; within healthy limits. This helps to balance a man. This helps a man to be more sensitive to the world and to women at large. A man is like dry hard earth, and a woman is like water. When he is too hard, she is able to quench the thirst and make the soil renewed and healthy again.

A woman is a beautiful creation. In my opinion, a woman is the most beautiful of creations ever created. In my humble opinion, she becomes less beautiful when she is opposite of her feminine nature.

I guess this is the new thing in our society; women that show no emotion and definitely not the emotion of love to their mate; highly testosterone filled women. Women that don't want to be touched, hugged, or kissed. Again, a man learns how to love from a woman. You have to be very careful of the foods you are eating and thoughts you are thinking. They change the chemical and hormonal makeup of your body, which ultimately change you. You may find your testosterone levels out of balance with the levels of estrogen.

You become what you think. When You Think Like a Man, You Act Like a Man. Meaning, there is no balance in the relationship. If the man is thinking and acting like a man, and you are as well, it basically

becomes two men in the relationship. One just looks like and has the anatomy of a female, but her actions and thoughts are that of a man. This doesn't work out so well for the long-term.

What also begins to happen is that the man becomes more and more docile to keep peace in the relationship. Therefore, he begins to act more like a woman because there is less feminine energy in the relationship. So, the woman begins to complain that he is NOT A MAN. He can't be if he wants to keep the relationship because the woman is being the WO-MAN.

If he doesn't become less aggressive or docile, he begins to become even more aggressive than normal. His talk will become more aggressive and his behaviors will as well. He will feel challenged as he would with a man, and will begin to draw certain invisible lines in conversation and territory. Because she is thinking like a man, he feels this energy she is giving off and will be on guard for a showdown. If he feels threatened his natural FIGHT or FLIGHT instincts will kick in.

#6 – The Adulterous Woman

The term, adulterous woman, is used numerous times in the book of Proverbs. So much so, that I had to fully examine the word adulterous and its use in each one of the scriptures that it was used.

According to Wikipedia, **adultery** is sexual intercourse between a married person and someone other than the spouse. It actually predates the establishment of Judaism, Christianity, Hinduism, and

Islam. In some cultures and societies it is considered a felony, and grounds to be sentenced to death.
Here is one part of what King Solomon had to say about the adulterous woman:

For the lips of the adulterous woman drip honey, and her speech is smoother than oil; but in the end she is bitter as gall (poison), sharp as a double-edged sword. Her feet go down to death; her steps lead straight to the grave. She gives no thought to the way of life; <u>her paths wander aimlessly, but she does not know it.</u>

I love the underlined part..."*Her paths wander aimlessly, but she does not know it.*"

I once was told by a pimp, "I've never met a woman that didn't need some direction. All women need some direction from a man at some point. It just depends on who actually ends up given them the directions, is where they'll end up going." Many women don't know they are sometimes wandering aimlessly.

There is no real goal. They are constantly making moves based on their emotions or on their newest whim. They can easily become like a man without a woman. They don't have any real direction or long-term ambitions other than work and career, if they even have that.

The following is the rest of what was said by King Solomon in the verses following those above:
Now then, my sons, listen to me; do not turn

aside from what I say. Keep to a path far from her, do not go near the door of her house, lest you lose your honor to others and your dignity to one who is cruel, lest strangers feast on your wealth and your toil enrich the house of another. At the end of your life you will groan, when your flesh and body are spent. You will say, "How I hated discipline! How my heart spurned correction! I would not obey my teachers or turn my ear to my instructors. And I was soon in serious trouble in the Assembly of God's people."

He goes on to remind the men of his time and those following for thousands of years to come***, "Do not lust in your heart after her beauty or let her <u>captivate</u> you with her eyes. For a prostitute can be had for a loaf of bread, but another man's wife preys on your very life."***

Run from a woman that is married and trying to get you to have sex with her. She is an adulterous woman. This is not safe or a wise thing to do.

#7 – The Woman that Can't Keep Her Feet at Home

The woman that always has to be out in public getting attention is not the woman that you will more than likely be pleased with as a wife. She has to have the attention of not just the public, but many times, other men.

She has a need to be in the face of other men and to receive attention from other men for no particular reason. Not for the purpose of conducting business or community service, but for her own need to have that attention. In many instances, she will play as if she is oblivious to it. Other times, it will be blatant "reckless eyeballing." What is reckless eyeballing? Reckless eyeballing originally came from when Blacks were having too much contact with a White person. Many times blacks were killed or beaten for this; especially if it was a black man towards a white woman. Well, in today's terms, it's when your man or woman is having too much eye contact with the opposite sex; especially while out with you. It is blatant disrespect and has the potential to cause a number of issues that are usually unwelcomed.

The two women that I dated the longest knew how to handle other men approaching them very well. They were not "reckless eyeballing" kind of women. So, I knew that if they were approached by a man, it was the man's doing. They would not give a man a sign or signal to approach them. If a guy would approach them, one of them would tell guys, "I don't have a phone." No matter what they would say, she would say, "I don't have a phone." She would also tell them, "I don't have a name." The other would just sit there and ignore them. If that didn't work, she would say "I'm happily married."

These were two women that I never had to worry about while we were dating if they were entertaining other men. Both of these women's mother and father were still married, and they had a decent relationship with their father. This may have played a role in them not being attention hungry during our relationship

from "male friends." I am all for males and females being friends. However, when in a relationship, the "male and/or female friend" needs to be introduced to the opposite sex, in order to help keep peace, produce long-term trust, and increase the possibility of the relationship actually lasting.

Read this story of the woman that couldn't keep her feet at home. It's from one of the greatest writers of all time, King Solomon.

The Woman that Couldn't Keep Her Feet at Home
By King Solomon

My son, keep my words, And treasure my commands within you. Keep my commands and live, And my law as the apple of your eye. Bind them on your fingers; Write them on the tablet of your heart. Say to wisdom, "You are my sister..."

And call understanding your nearest kin, That they may keep you from the immoral woman, From the seductress who flatters with her words.

For at the window of my house I looked through my lattice, and saw among the simple, I perceived among the youths, a young man devoid of understanding, passing along the street near her corner; and he took the path to her house in the twilight, in the evening, in the black and dark night. And there a woman met him, with the attire of a harlot, and a crafty heart.

She was loud and rebellious; her feet would not stay at home.

At times she was outside, at times in the open square, Lurking at every corner. So she caught him and kissed him; With an impudent face she said to him:
"I have peace offerings with me; Today I have paid my vows.

So I came out to meet you, diligently to seek your face, And I have found you. I have spread my bed with tapestry, Colored coverings of Egyptian linen. I have perfumed my bed with myrrh, aloes, and cinnamon. Come, let us take our fill of love until morning; Let us delight ourselves with love.

For my husband is not at home; He has gone on a long journey; He has taken a bag of money with him,
And will come home on the appointed day."
With her enticing speech she caused him to yield, with her flattering lips she seduced him.

Immediately he went after her, as an ox goes to the slaughter, Or as a fool to the correction of the stocks, till an arrow struck his liver. As a bird hastens to the snare, He did not know it would cost his life.

Now therefore, listen to me, my children; Pay attention to the words of my mouth:
Do not let your heart turn aside to her ways, Do not stray into her paths; For she has cast down many wounded, And all who were slain by her were strong men.

Her house is the way to hell, descending to the chambers of death.

#8 – The Foolish Woman

A Foolish Woman is clamorous; she is simple and knows nothing. This is from chapter 9 of the Book of Proverbs. The word *clamorous* is synonymous with loud, obnoxious, and chaotic noise. It's the kind of noise that children would make for the purpose of getting attention or to get on someone's nerves. Meaning, a foolish woman is synonymous with being loud, obnoxious, and attention hungry.

A Foolish Woman would be considered one who does not understand the basics of life. She doesn't understand how to conduct herself in public or in private; especially around the opposite sex. Not because she can't understand them or hasn't had anyone to teach her, but because she rejected knowledge, wisdom, and understanding when it was presented to her. Many of the men and women reading this may reject this knowledge; for whatever reason they choose to do so. However, in the book of Hosea, destruction is the penalty for rejecting knowledge.

In chapter 9 of Proverbs, King Solomon continues to speak about the Foolish Woman when he goes on to say, *And as for him that lacks understanding, she says to him, "Stolen water is sweet, and bread eaten in secret is pleasant."*

Only a foolish woman would say something like this. And only a man that had no understanding or had not been taught the ways of life would be fooled by this. At times, love can blind a man from recognizing the Foolish Woman.

The Foolish Woman, like the adulterous woman, will easily lead you on paths of death and destruction.

If you are dating a Foolish Woman, recognize her as such, and it may be very wise to run.

#9 – The Woman that Lacks Discretion

According to Google, discretion is a noun that means; ***the quality of behaving or speaking in such a way as to avoid causing offense or revealing private information.***

A woman that lacks discretion doesn't have to be a gossip or a liar. She may be telling the truth about all that she is saying; however, she is usually revealing information that should be kept secret for her own protection and the protection of others.

A woman that is not discreet usually has no life and has no shame. The other way to look at a woman that has no discretion is a woman that cannot keep her body or sex life private. She usually styles herself like a harlot or seductress. She probably knows that this is not an acceptable behavior and just may enjoy doing it because of this.

As her man, she will usually bring trouble to your doorstep because she will draw sexually hungry men to her and the wrong kind of attention to both of you.

King Solomon says, *"As a ring of gold in a swine's snout, So is a lovely woman that lacks discretion."* ~Proverbs 11:22

No matter how lovely she is, she loses the loveliness about herself when she lacks discretion. I recently posted some of my thoughts about this on my Facebook wall.

I had to explain this to women; "When you post pictures of yourself taking pictures of your butt, your breast, and multiple erotic photos, you decrease your chances of getting a man to appreciate you and actually take you serious. You decrease the possibility of finding a man that actually wants you for you and not for your body. Then, when your status updates say one thing, but your pictures say something totally different, you are confusing the good men. You look hungry for attention, unstable emotionally, and confused about where you are in life. Are you trying to be married and be in a serious relationship? Or do you want to still party, be promiscuous, and single?"

Well, a few of them found this a little condescending. So, I had to further explain it to them like this; "If I, or any man, was constantly putting pictures of myself with no shirt on or the imprint of my penis, would you take me seriously and want to marry me?"

They understood me then. I I did this, I would be considered as a man without discretion. They may want to have sex with me or look at me as "eye candy," but not as a man that was actually ready to get married and have a family. Well, the same goes for a woman.

King Solomon says, ***"Discretion will preserve you."***

He further says, "***An excellent wife is the crown of her husband, but she who causes shame is like rottenness in his bones.***" She usually will cause him shame due to her lack of discreet behavior, words, actions, and/or style of dress.

If you are dating a woman that has no discretion, it may be very wise to run from her.

#10 – The Harlot & Seductress

"For by means of a harlot, a man is reduced to a crust of bread." I really don't have to go further. This one sentence explains anything that I could add to it. King Solomon asked for wisdom, and wisdom is what he received.

There are those that will argue the fact that all women trade sex for money. However, a prostitute or harlot is a woman that trades sex for money as a profession. She is also by all means a seductress. She has to be in order to receive payment for something that a man should be able to get from his wife as a mutually beneficial act; however, even married men that may be having sex with his wife on a regular basis actually go and pay for sex from a prostitute or give their money to a woman dancing on a pole.

A harlot or seductress, in most cases, has become so used to sex that she does it as a habit. Much like a drug. I was watching a documentary about 7-10 years ago on prostitution. The woman said, "I'm so numb to sex. I don't even enjoy it anymore. Lubrication is a must for me." It had become all about money and whatever she needed to do to get the money.

The seductress of today's time would be more like the stripper, or the woman that will give something to you for the sole purpose of getting money from you. The stripper is quite interesting. She is a seductive entertainer. I've sold many books outside the strip clubs. Over the years, I have been able to have many conversations with many women that strip. Many of them don't like men. Not all, but some have been sexually abused and molested and see this as a way of getting back at men by taking their money or getting attention that they never had from men.

While most of them don't have sex with the clients that frequent the strip clubs, some of them do. I've watched young ladies lose what was left of their minds doing this for a living. While others, made money and let the lifestyle become the lifestyle they embraced.

Then, there are those that go back and forth. They use it as a means to an end, but they keep using it over and over as the means to a "never-ending end." Either way, there are men that will throw thousands of dollars to see a woman shake her butt and show her breasts.

Marriages have been totally destroyed behind prostitutes and seductresses. If you are dating a prostitute or a seductress, it would be in your best interest to run. You are putting yourself in a situation that can easily become a never-ending cycle that has NO EXIT PLAN.

5 Men You Should Never Marry

This chapter came about due to the previous chapter. It is also based on WISDOM from King Solomon. It is a very important chapter for women that are seeking to get married. It will save you from the wrong kind of man. It will help you develop a better relationship with the man you currently date, if you use the information here to motivate and encourage him.

I am and think I will forever be the type of man that understands the POWER of LOVE from a woman. It can literally change a man and take him into his destiny. If you're a man or woman reading this book, I hope that it will help you make a better selection of a mate in marriage and dating.

The late Napoleon Hill, one of the bestselling authors in the last 100+ years wrote a book he entitled ***Think and Grow Rich***. In the book, he had a list of the 30 Causes of Failure. On the list, one of the reasons is "WRONG SELECTION OF A MATE IN MARRIAGE." He further states, *"This is a most common cause of failure. The relationship of marriage brings people intimately into contact. Unless the relationship is harmonious, failure is likely to follow. Moreover, it will be a form of failure that is marked by misery and unhappiness, destroying all signs of ambition."* He studied for 25 years to come up with the principles of success and true wealth. He personally interviewed and studied the greatest men of his time. Let's begin shall we...

#1 – A Lazy Man

There is a difference between a lazy man and a man that may have fallen on hard times, or works but doesn't make a lot of money. Sometimes, women get the latter two confused with a lazy man.

A lazy man and a man with a dream can be the same man. However, they usually aren't. You also have the lazy dreamer. The lazy dreamer sits around and doesn't act on anything that they ever say they want to accomplish. They make excuses why they can't get started, why they can't find work, why no one will buy or support their product or service that they don't even have available, and other excuses. The lazy dreamer lacks the mental toughness to actually think through

the process, make a plan and start going towards it.

They relate pain with actually taking action. It is too much pain to actually ask someone for help with the things they don't know how to do. It is so much better to just dream about it in their mind as opposed to moving towards the desire of their heart.

I finally realized why a lazy dreamer does this; it allows them to continue to talk about something that hasn't been produced because in the producing of the thing, it will take a lot of mental, emotional, and physical change on their behalf.

Let's see what King Solomon has to say about the Lazy Man.

Proverbs 10:26 As vinegar to the teeth and smoke to the eyes, So is the **lazy** man to those who send him.

Proverbs 12:24 The hand of the diligent will rule, But the **lazy** man will be put to forced labor.

Proverbs 12:27 The **lazy** man does not roast what he took in hunting, But diligence is man's precious possession.

Proverbs 13:4 The soul of a **lazy** man desires, and has nothing; But the soul of the diligent shall be made rich.

Proverbs 15:19 The way of the **lazy** man is like a hedge of thorns, But the way of the upright is a highway.

Proverbs 19:24 A **lazy** man buries his hand in the bowl, And will not so much as bring it to his mouth again.

Proverbs 20:4 The **lazy** man will not plow because of winter; He will beg during harvest and have nothing.

Proverbs 21:25 The desire of the **lazy** man kills him, For his hands refuse to labor.

Proverbs 22:13 The **lazy** man says, "There is a lion outside! I shall be slain in the streets!"

Proverbs 24:30-31 I went by the field of the lazy *man*, And by the vineyard of the man devoid of understanding; And there it was, all overgrown with thorns; Its surface was covered with nettles; Its stone wall was broken down.

As we can see, there is nothing good said about the lazy man. These are only 10 examples, Solomon was a King who interacted and led thousands of men. Therefore, he had to know men. He is said to be the richest and wisest man to walk the earth. He was so rich that some say in today's time he would have been financially worth TRILLIONS of dollars.

Unless you want to work while you are young and when you are old, you should never marry a lazy man. Michele Obama held her fair share of financial responsibility of the family for a long time. She was rather stable prior to getting married. Although Barack didn't make a lot of money and was a dreamer, he was not a lazy dreamer. She saw characteristics of a

visionary that was working towards his vision. I don't think that she'll ever have to work again. His work ethic, although not highly paid when he was younger, prepared him for his position as the leader of the Free World.

#2 – The Habitual Liar

Men are really not good liars. I think we usually get caught. So, if you get caught in your lies I don't think that qualifies you as a good liar. We lie usually to protect ourselves or the woman we love. Just know, *"There is not a just man that does good; and does not sin."* This was also said by King Solomon. When I first read this I understood it. A man, no matter how just and honest he is, if it comes down to protecting himself and his family, he will more than likely not tell the whole truth.

However, the difference between this guy and a habitual liar is that his lies have become his whole identity. He has told the same lies for so long that even he believes his own lies. In a relationship, depending on the woman he is with, he has created a story to fit each woman's ideal man. I often hear women say, "But I believed he was telling the truth."

One of the female survey respondents wrote: ***"An untruthful man is by far the worst. That includes lying, cheating." (9/30/2012 7:35 AM)*** A man can be married, engaged, on the down low, and everything else; but if he can make a woman believe that she is the only one, he is in her mind. Once the lie is in the mind it is hard to believe the truth. What goes into the mind first is usually what the mind thinks is right or correct. This is the same way that a close friend can plant a seed in the mind of a woman, and have her sleep with him. A woman can easily do the same. It doesn't even have to be true. It just has to sound believable, and look somewhat believable.

Therefore, a man that will habitually lie to you and to his own self about things that are not true, will lead you and your household to paths of destruction. It is a game to many men that are habitual liars. They get a kick out of lying and leading others astray. One must be able to make peace with where they are and who they are and come clean.

Even those that consider themselves to be non-believers in any of the major religions of the world or a supreme creator understand that a habitual liar is not a desirable person to have around.

You must know the intention and reason when a person tells a lie. You must allow them to be able to tell the truth to you without consequence in order to curb them from the habit of lying. Otherwise, DO NOT marry a man that is a habitual liar.

#3 – The Unfaithful Man

"Most men will proclaim each his own goodness, but Who Can Find a Faithful Man?" I tell women all the time, "***If you find a man that is faithful to you, it is in your best interest to keep him.***" The other things about him that you may not like are traits that can be improved. An unfaithful man is usually unfaithful in many other areas of his life as well. You

can see this early on if you are able to pay attention to the signs.

An unfaithful man is much like the Adulterous woman. The unfaithful man can have children outside of the relationship, catch and STD and bring it back to his woman that has been faithful to him, and he can torment you with years of agonizing encounters from other women. A woman that wants your man because she has been told by him that he doesn't love you will do almost anything to destroy your relationship. And when I say anything I mean almost anything.

Plain and simply put, if you are with an unfaithful man, the only way he will ever learn is to seek professional help. Being sexually unfaithful can become a habit. In order for the habit to be broken, one must seek outside help. If it is that bad and you love the guy that much and can forgive him, if you stay, you must know that without the professional help, he is more than likely not going to change anytime soon.

It may be in your best interest to do yourself and him a favor and keep it moving. Even Pimpin' Ken said on Black Men Revealed, *"If you're trying to bring other people into your marriage, that's not a marriage and ain't no reason to be married."*

"But the soul of the unfaithful feeds on violence."
From Proverbs 13:2 ~NKJV~

#4 – A Man who hates Wisdom, Understanding, Knowledge, and Instruction

A man that hates wisdom hates women. A man that hates women hates himself. King Solomon didn't say this, Armani Valentino did. (smile) Wisdom has been hidden in the woman. A woman is a man and a woman's first teacher; in the womb. So, the first instruction comes from a woman.

The ultimate goal of life is to become one with LOVE. A man first learns how to LOVE from a woman. If there is no love, there can be no TRUE WISDOM. Wisdom comes from The MOST HIGH, and you cannot have wisdom without knowledge and understanding because WISDOM IS THE CORRECT USE OF KNOWLEDGE. Ultimately meaning, you can't have either of these without instruction. A woman is our first teacher, and we as men are taught to deal with a woman according to KNOWLEDGE.

Proverbs is often referred to as the Book of Wisdom. It has 31 chapters, and the 31st chapter has 31 verses. Luqman, The 31st chapter of the Qu'ran, is also known as the Book of Wisdom. The number 4 is said to represent *foundation*. In building and construction the square is a very common shape used for foundations. There are 4 corners of a square. If we look at the number 31, we will see that the sum of 3+1 = 4.

Therefore, after being INSTRUCTED in KNOWLEDGE one gains UNDERSTANDING. Once understanding is gained and the knowledge can be used correctly; this is considered to be WISDOM. The goal is to have a WISE-DOME. Without it, one will continue in

circles and never understand the reasons & seasons of life. When a man understands the reasons & seasons of life, he is able to better prepare for each season and able to help himself and others navigate the storms of life more smoothly.

The question is asked by King Solomon, *"Why is there in the hand of a fool, the purchase price of wisdom, since he has no heart for it?"* Wisdom is not for a fool because to give or sell wisdom to a fool, only creates a wise fool. He becomes wise in his own eyes. I used to hear the old folks say, "There is no fool like an old fool." In Proverbs 19:20 King Solomon writes, **Listen to counsel and receive instruction, that you may be wise in your latter days.**

My 9th Grade English Teacher & I didn't see Eye-to-Eye

This causes me to remember the importance of my 9th grade English teacher, Ms. Howell, who made us write 15 minutes a day. Ms. Howell and I DID NOT usually see eye-to-eye because I thought I knew too much sometimes (smile), but I sure do appreciate her for doing this. It forced us to not have writers block. At that time, I loved writing poetry and had been published in a book of poetry. I didn't necessarily like to write fiction or non-fiction, but I eventually submitted to the instruction and begin to express myself better and better.

The process of writing for these 15 minutes became easier and easier. She later told us, "Most people won't read every day. But even fewer will write every day. Later in life, it will help you to express yourself." I didn't see myself as a writer then, nor do I see myself as a writer now. However, I do see myself as someone that likes to express himself, and I love for others to do the same. The more ways you have to express yourself, the more opportunities for you to express yourself will be made available for you. You may even begin to get paid for doing so.

Although we didn't always see eye-to-eye, I must say that I sure do appreciate her now. She was right. I on the other hand had no clue what the world was going to be like after high school. I'm glad that I was able to listen and be somewhat obedient to instruction.

Had I not listened to her and many other instructors, teachers, and men and women that took time to show me the right path I would be saying the exact words written in Proverbs 5:12-14 (NKJV); *And say: "How I have hated instruction, And my heart despised correction! I have not obeyed the voice of my teachers, nor inclined my ear to those who instructed me! I was on the verge of total ruin, In the midst of the assembly and congregation."*

A man who hates Wisdom, Understanding, Knowledge, and Instruction is a man that will not be able to lead or follow. He is not a man that will rise to the great heights in his selected area of life. Even a drug dealer, if he is to be a good drug dealer, he must listen to learn the rules of the game he is in. A preacher that wants to be great must do the same thing. The paths of

success always leave trails. Conversely, so have the paths of failure.

"And *those* who are *wise* shall shine like
the brightness of the sky above..."
From Daniel 12:3 (NIV)

#5 – The Man Who Rejoices in Evil and is Quick to Anger

I learned not to be quick to anger as a very young child. I saw what anger caused people to do and say to one another. At the age of two years old, my mother and father got into an argument that caused someone to bring a gun over. I believe it was one of my father's sisters. Either way, the gun went off while my sister and I were sitting on the top of the car witnessing all of this, and the bullet was heading straight towards the both of us. All of the sudden the bullet slowed down and moved in front of us; much like the movie The Matrix. When I first saw this movie on my 19th birthday, I was in awe because I had actually witnessed this same thing in my own life as a very young child.

It was at that point where I knew to always try and talk things out with people as opposed to resulting to violence. I would see more violence from other people where I grew up. I acted violently one time in school and never did again. Earlier this year, I was at the church that I was baptized in as a child and that generations of my family have been members of, and told the following story.

A little boy and I were in our kindergarten class. Something happened that allowed him to be able to get my quarter. I asked him multiple times to give me my quarter back. He refused. I realized that he had no plans to give me my quarter. There was no teacher in the classroom at this time so I had no one to handle the situation. I believe she had stepped away to the office.

So, I took matters into my own hands. I put him in the headlock and started choking the little boy. Now, I wasn't trying to hurt him, but I wanted my quarter. As I was doing this, all of the sudden the Principal came to the door and saw me. Needless to say, I was immediately told to let him go and come to office. I got the worst paddling ever. I think I may have only gotten one other paddling in my entire schooling. The paddling saved me from being an out of control child.

The Sunday that I told this story, the Principal, Mr. Austin, was there. I thanked him for helping me to be slow to anger. I appreciated him because he walked in on me and let me know that this was not the way to handle situations.

Learning to be slow to anger has always helped me tremendously. I am not nor will I ever say that I don't get angry. I believe that it is impossible to never ever get angry. And it may also be a little unhealthy. Even Christ got angry. I always have to remind people of this.

Proverbs 16:32 says, ***"He who is slow to anger is better than the mighty. And he who rules his (own) spirit (better) than he who takes a city."*** Being able to control your anger is POWER!

"An angry man stirs up strife, and
a furious man abounds in transgression."
Proverbs 29:22 ~NKJV~

I learned that life will teach you the hard way or the easy way. The hard way is to learn on your own without guidance or counsel. The evil men that have walked the earth have always seemed to be first accompanied by quick tempers. They were not helped by anyone as little boys to control their temper and to only act on their anger of emotion when absolutely necessary. Therefore, many a genius has never become known to the world because they were not able to control their anger and it grew, which ended their lives either in prison, insane asylums, or 6 feet under.

"You will know a tree by the fruit it bears." A bad tree at the root will not bear a whole lot of good fruit. The way you start doesn't always determine how you will end, but it is a good indicator of your potential end.

You must be able to see a man for who he is. Anger management works. Everyone has triggers and those triggers can be suppressed through retraining of the mind. I often tell people "Professional counseling and hypnotherapy work wonders."

Children and adults must have healthy outlets and activities to curb their anger. Whatever may be said about public school, it has saved many of people's lives because outside of school millions of children had no life and no one that cared about them. It gave them hope.

Anger is usually expressed and acted upon when a person feels powerless and wants to get their power back in a particular situation. Many times, it has been lying dormant. However, a person that is always angry or angry more than a few times a year needs to seek professional help. They need someone to talk to and they need some activities before the anger turns into evil doings.

If you are dating a man that rejoices in evil and is quick to anger, it is not in your best interest to marry him.

19

What Men Want What Women Need

This is always a question or statement that men and women around the world bring up. I have noticed that there are very few things when it comes to relationships that seem to hold true across the board. Everyone has their opinion about this and about that, but few statements and research hold 90% for male/female relationships.

Women want to be independent. Men want to be independent. Men want freedom. Women want freedom. Men want respect. Women want respect. Men want love. Women want love. We all want pretty much the same things.

We often argue about the issues. If both parties could hear one another from totally objective standpoints, they would see they are usually wanting or complaining about the same things. The methodology of giving or receiving these seems to be the real issue.

Women have to remember, "We are not you. Don't try and make us be you. Enjoy us as the wonderful creatures that we were made to be. We only want to be respected. In doing so, you'll be happier and we'll be happier too."

Men have to remember, "Don't try and understand or change a woman. She is who she is. She is wonderfully and beautifully made. We are only asked to love them. When we love them, they will almost always return the same or greater."

In short, *if you get nothing else from this book*, I want you to get one of the only TRUTHS that I have seen stand across racial, religious, and socio-economic backgrounds:

Women need to FEEL WANTED.

AND...

Men want to FEEL NEEDED.

BUT...

Women NEED to feel wanted for something other than **SEX**.

AND...

Men WANT to feel needed for something other than **MONEY**.

When the two people in a relationship can totally understand this and love one another unconditionally, it makes everything else so much easier.

Below is a poem that I want you and your partner to memorize and say every day. It's really powerful and has helped thousands learn to LOVE WITHOUT LIMITS.

TODAY
By Armani Valentino

Today I will BELIEVE.
Today I remove ALL Fear & Doubt
From my MIND & HEART.

Today I will be THANKFUL,
And LIVE in a constant state of APPRECIATION.

Today I will LOVE WITHOUT LIMITS.
Today I will be the LOVE I DESIRE.

Today is ALL I HAVE.
Therefore, I WILL LOVE TODAY.

CONCLUSION

In conclusion, if you want to be married, I hope that you will take the responsibility of marriage seriously. It is as some people say, "A Ministry of its own." The family is important, and I believe it is the backbone of any nation.

Having been raised in a single parent home, no matter how things may have appeared, it was a struggle for my mother, and the negative effects still affect me and my sisters today. Statistically speaking, we've beat some but not all of the odds.

As we go into the many years ahead, I would love to see more and more women and men focused on becoming better individuals and less concerned with pointing the finger at their mate. It would be great for more and more successful couples to speak up and be open and transparent on the benefits of marriage. There are plenty of examples of why not to be married. Maybe a better balance on television and in the communities across the country would help.

To the women: You are the mothers of mother earth. If you are not nurturing, loving, caring, gentle and kind, then there can be none of this on the earth. Please focus more on your inner self and connect with that source of love within. It will help the whole world heal. But the world cannot heal without their being a mass healing and restoration in you.

We love you, but have to be taught how to love by you! WE have messed up for generations as a whole, but

until LOVE IS RESTORED in the hearts of women, the world cannot heal.

You are the essential key to unlocking the mysteries. Use your feminine energy in politics, government, education & schools, business, healthcare, and anywhere else. Most of all use it at home. A happy home starts with a happy woman. Be happy within yourself and your whole environment will adjust to you. Choose to be happy on a daily basis regardless of the circumstances because life is fleeting, and time is the one thing we can't get back.

Love the man in your life. Understand that many times other women; as much as they may have good intentions, they are not the man in your life. As opposed to trying to define yourself through your INDEPENDENCE look more towards a new path of INTERDEPENDENCE.

To the men: We are at a crossroads in history where the tendency to feel powerless in our families and communities is a real concern. Our egos are being challenged and checked on a regular basis. Our ability to deal with the stress and demands of providing for our family are constantly being compared to that of other men. The constant cries for more and more are real. It is a challenge. Be humble yet confident that everything will be okay. You are not superman, but you are a man. Don't neglect yourself to the point of giving up. Violence against yourself and others is not the solution. As the great poet wrote "REST IF YOU MUST, BUT DON'T YOU QUIT!"

The more we understand and educate ourselves as men, the more we will be able to meet the challenges that are sure to come. Decisions must be made. We must become single minded and focused. Make the decision to love, care for, and be present for our families. Be single minded on showing up for the game of life. LOVE is sometimes hard. BUT...The better we become at learning how to love, the better we will become at LOVE.

Let's set new standards for our conduct amongst ourselves, women, and children. If things are to get better, we must get better! WE can be more. WE can do more.

Trust that marriage will shape us into the men that we see ourselves becoming. Trust the process. Trust that a woman is just as important to the world as we are. Empower a woman, and in doing so you ultimately empower yourself and the whole world. In the words of Minister Louis Farrakhan, "A nation can rise no higher than its woman."

In closing, Hate only produces more hate,
but LOVE CONQUERS ALL.

JUST LOVE...

Special Thanks to:

First and foremost the MOST HIGH.

My mother, I appreciate you and love you very much for all that you have instilled in me. Your sacrifices I can never repay. To My late Great Grandparents, thank you for allowing me to see a good picture of what LOVE was all about. To my two sisters, Gerre' and Chesa. Thank you for the couch, the food, and all the craziness we have endured through the years. To my four nephews, Jabriel, Marques, Brian, & Kaemon, I love each of you and I 'm anticipating great things from each of you. I'm here for you. To my Grandma, aunts & uncles, and cousins, I LOVE YOU!

To all those that helped me in multiple ways during the last phase of this book I am grateful and you are appreciated: Kimberly "Baby Doll", Tajuana, Cherese, Demetra, Kelland, Carlos, Victor & Bab and The Adetiba family. Sam & Julia Wright, Pam W., Prophet & Prophetess Johnson, Chris Bivens, Elders Rufus & Glenda Fields, & Pastor Kenneth Reid for all the prayers and conversations. The Office Machines, Inc. Family; especially Kevin, Nelson, Gina, Virginia, Levi & Juliet you all have been family and kept me from giving up more than you know.

To everyone else I may have forgotten thank you! If you ever bought a book, read/sent an email, attended a play, movie screening, gave me words of encouragement, prayed for me, or just wanted to see me reach the highest of heights, I appreciate you!

Thanks to the radio & television stations, newspapers, churches, colleges, mosques, book clubs, businesses, bookstores, and civic organizations that have brought me in to speak, and to help someone through my words. You are greatly appreciated.

And last but not least, to my son, Armani Christian Valentino, I love you and I am looking forward to being a great father to you. At the time of this publication, you just spoke your first words, "Dada! Dada! DADA!"

Claim the INCREASE! See you all at the TOP!

www.ingramcontent.com/pod-product-compliance
Lightning Source LLC
Chambersburg PA
CBHW031158270326
41931CB00006B/317